The Ocean in the Sand

JAPAN:

FROM LANDSCAPE

TO GARDEN

MARK HOLBORN

The Ocean in the Sand

JAPAN: FROM LANDSCAPE TO GARDEN

SHAMBHALA · BOULDER · 1978

Shambhala Publications, Inc.
1123 Spruce Street
Boulder, Colorado 80302

Distributed in the United States by Random House and in
Canada by Random House of Canada Ltd.

Printed in Great Britain
Display lettering by Tim Holloway
Designed by Peter Guy

Contents

Acknowledgements

I would like to acknowledge my debt to Lorraine Kuck for *The World of the Japanese Garden*, particularly for her work on Chinese gardens, and to Teiji Itoh, whose work with the photographers Takeji Iwamiya and Yukio Futagawa, has been a constant source of inspiration.

I am especially indebted to Takeji Iwamiya, Mark Haworth-Booth, Tetsuya and Kazuko Uehara and to friends from County Kilkenny to Suwa-no-se, without whom this book would not have been possible.

I would like to thank the following for illustrations:
Cambridge University Press, The National Museum, Tokyo, The Victoria and Albert Museum, London, The Japanese Embassy, London, Yukio Futagawa, Yoichi Midorikawa and Takeji Iwamiya.

In cases where I have quoted from the books mentioned in the bibliography an asterisk appears alongside the title. In each case I would like to acknowledge with thanks the publisher and the author of the book

List of Illustrations

The real treasure, that which can put an end to our poverty and all our trials, is never very far; there is no need to seek it in a distant country. It lies buried in the most intimate parts of our own house; that is, of our own being. It is behind the stove, the centre of the life and warmth that rule our existence, the heart, if only we knew how to unearth it. And yet—there is this strange and persistent fact, that it is only after a pious journey in a distant region, in a new land, that the meaning of that inner voice guiding us on our search can make itself understood by us.

Heinrich Zimmer
as quoted by Mircea Eliade in
Myths, Dreams and Mysteries

There is nothing more pleasant and instructive than to immerse yourself in the society of people of an entirely different race, whom you respect, with whom you sympathise, of whom you are, though a stranger, proud. The Armenians' fullness of life, their rough tenderness, their noble inclination for hard work, their inexplicable aversion for any kind of metaphysics, and their splendid intimacy with the world of real things—all this said to me: you're awake, don't be afraid of your own time, don't be sly.

Wasn't this because I found myself among people, renowned for their teeming activity, who nevertheless told time not by the railroad station or the office clock, but by the sundial, such as the one I saw among the ruins of Zvartots in the form of the zodiac or of a rose inscribed in stone?

Osip Mandelstam
Journey to Armenia

Landscape, Season and Myth

Japan appears like a newly-risen island. The mountains surface sheer from the sea, as if suddenly thrust up from the ocean bed by some colossal force. The first view is as of virgin land. I wake to see the sunrise over Tsugaro Kaikyu, the straits between Hokkaido and Honshu. It is December, the sky is very clear. Stub-bowed fishing boats rise and fall from view behind the waves; the blue of their hulls is the blue of the sea and the sky. Passing close to the northern shore, the snow-capped peaks above the water and the curve of their slopes stir the memory of an early dream of mountain tops piercing the clouds, which swirl at their feet like the spray of a stormy sea; it is an image that recurs many times and will be imprinted on the imagination. From this distance of three or four miles, the land conforms to one's preconceptions. The mountains rise like islands in a sea of sky.

The coastline is rugged and scarred as if hammered and shattered into existence. It is scattered with small islands, some no bigger than boulders like giant stepping-stones, others green with shrubbery or the occasional solitary pine tree. Torn cliffs, jagged bays and twisted strata change to rolling, white dunes or the sand of grey, volcanic lava-flow. There is a rhythm in the broken shapes of deep caves and natural bridges. It is a violent rhythm; the rhythm of earthquake and volcano.

Entering Tokyo Bay, lighthouses are silhouetted against a flat skyline, like the hulls of spacecraft on launching-pads. Bridges link islands to the mainland and sleek tankers nose out into the Pacific. It is difficult to estimate a scale, for there is an element of unreality. It is like looking at an architectural model of some city of the future. The illusion vanishes abruptly as the clear, blue sky changes to a grey-brown haze that hangs heavily. The transition is sudden and extreme.

*   *   *

Mountains account for more than three-quarters of the total land mass of Japan. They run like a spine along the arc of the four main islands, forcing the Japanese out to the coasts and the sea. Densely-forested hills rise sharply from the plains. Every available flat area is

[11]

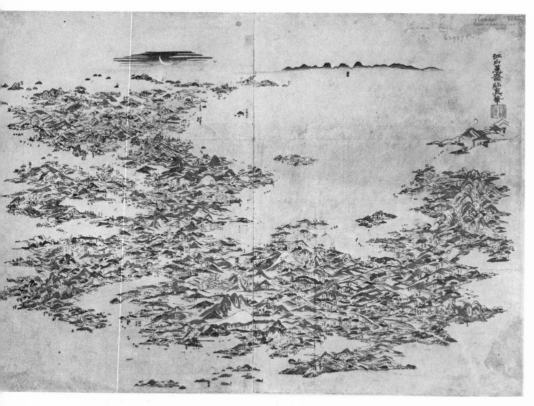

intensively cultivated, usually for rice. Any bare, unfor-
ested hillside is terraced with characteristic industry to
form extraordinary patterns in the earth. Tiers of rice
fields have been cut like enormous steps, that follow the
contours of the winding slopes. The terraces reflect the
industrious qualities of the people who made them. This
industry and energy can be seen in a different context
in the devastation of a landscape, as a result of the transition from the ashes of a defeated nation in the aftermath
of war to an economic superpower.

If you travel south from Tokyo down the Pacific
coast of Honshu, along one of the most highly-in-
dustrialised coastlines in the world, where 'red tides' in
the sea kill all marine life, you pass through cities where
passers-by collapse on the streets due to photochemical
smog and housewives buy oxygen in department stores.
Then you could be blinded by the apparent contradic-
tion that this is the same country where people experienced Nature with a harmony that was unique. They
strove not to conquer the hillside, but to move with it
and follow its curve like the flow of a river.

With the exception of the northern island, Hokkaido,
Japan lies in the temperate zone. The semi-tropical
climate of the south contrasts with the subzero tempera-
tures of Hokkaido in winter. The warm Japan current
runs along the Pacific coasts on the east, and on the west
the coasts of the Sea of Japan feel the Okhotsk current.
The cold winds from Siberia bring deep snow in winter,
and as a consequence the west coast of Honshu is known
as the Snow Country. The temperate climate of Japan
in summer and the heavy rainfall produce dense forests
and abundant vegetation. The moisture often hangs in
a low mist over the mountains, veiling the forested hills
in a subdued light.

Shifting from raging storms and Siberian winds to
the still calm of tropical heat, the seasonal extremes and
their cycle mark a flow to which the people are closely
attuned. Their lives revolve around the changes in
which they find a balance as striking as that of the landscape itself.

The winter snowfall is heavy on Hokkaido and the
west coast of Honshu; on the east coast and Kyushu,
the winter days are crisp and dry, the sky clear and blue.

[12]

In February, the first blossom of the Japanese apricot appears, and in late March the arrival of spring is marked by a burst of colour as the cherry trees flower; the first to bloom is the Spring Equinox cherry, higan sakura. The day of the spring equinox is set aside as one of the most important national holidays in the Japanese calendar. Specifically designated for the enjoyment of the season, the holiday celebrates the continuity of the cycle and the renewal of the life force after the decay of autumn and winter. Even the inhabitants of modern Tokyo delight in the blossom, which they view with the excitement of a great national event.

The temporary nature of the blossom, the power with which it arrives and the speed with which it vanishes, holds a certain appeal for the Japanese. The life of the samurai was proverbially compared to the short-lived blossom: 'the cherry among flowers is like the samurai among men'. However, this exuberant appreciation for the flower and the season has now taken on proportions which rather than reinforcing a tradition have become sentimental and clichéd. Down many Tokyo streets pink, plastic petals are displayed on street lamps and telegraph poles permanently as if to tell one that every day is spring. As the modern city grows, the inhabitants become more insulated from the seasons and the awareness of the cycle is diminished. The plastic flowers stand out as a gesture intended to fix the flow and halt the very transience that lies deep in the Japanese imagination.

With the coming of the rains from the south, which reach central Japan in June, the spring passes to summer. Then the lush summer greenery of the deciduous trees, the Japanese oak, the chestnut, birch and elm, stands out from the darker shades of the coniferous forests. The heat of summer can be fierce and uncomfortable, but at night when the screens of the houses are drawn fully open, the Japanese can be enveloped by the warm air of the season. Sei Shonagon, a lady of the Heian court of the tenth century, opened her Pillow Book by describing the most beautiful qualities of each season,

In summer, the nights. Not only when the moon shines down, but on dark nights too, when the fireflies flit to and fro, and even when it rains, how beautiful it is.

In September, the heat of summer is kindled into wild storms; the typhoons strike inland bringing torrential rain in the driving wind. As the gentle, forested slopes change to the jagged peak of the volcano, so too does the season change from the restrained calm of the summer evenings to the violence of the typhoon, when the full force of Nature is unleashed.

In the wake of the storms comes the quiet of autumn, rich with a poignancy to which the Japanese are particularly sensitive. The autumn mood, with the falling of the leaves and the baring of the trees, emphasises the transient world. The Japanese have projected the natural decay of the season on to the human condition and link the autumn images, like the red leaves of the maples that carpet the ground, with partings, bereavements and above all, solitude. The power of the season of death is strangely fertile, for it contains the beauty of suggestion; the image of autumn and its accompanying decay implies a future growth and flowering. The mood of solitude is inseparable from the image, for through solitude, the Japanese have realised the flow of Nature. This flow is reflected in aesthetic taste, but more than that—it beats in the very pulse of their vitality.

The Japanese imagination is infused with the balance of the extremes of the landscape and the striking definition of the season. Time is gauged in the passing season, which provides the context of the literary and aesthetic image. Japanese artists and writers have attempted to capture the sense of moment in the mood of the season; their images acquired depth when they reflected the flow; the moment was potent when its transience was implied. Consequently much of Japanese art is the art of suggestion, not the art of representation.

Throughout its history, Japanese literature has mirrored the changing forces and extremes of Nature; the Manyoshu, the eighth-century collection of poems, the literature of the Heian court, the poetic forms of 'tanka' and 'haiku', all contain imagery rooted in the mountains, forest and sea, and in the passing season. The particular qualities of the different seasons were communally expressed in poetry parties, which during the Heian period were conducted by the court with great ritual as popular contests. The violence of the medieval warriors of Japan and the destruction of the later civil wars only emphasised the delicacy of the balance of human life; it was understandable therefore that the Japanese continued to identify with the changing natural cycle and measured their lives with an image as transitory as the bloom and decay of a flower.

Study of the Pillow Book of Sei Shonagon reveals how closely the Heian court observed the changing season and the great importance they attached to the calendar; the festivals of the modern calendar demonstrate how the tradition has survived. But there is another key to the source of this sense of identity with the natural world, that has its origins in an archaic and intuitive knowledge and demonstrates both the flow and balance of landscape and season most explicitly. The key can be found in the garden.

Religious veneration is still an active part of the Japanese experience of Nature. Through Shinto, 'the way of the gods', the natural elements have been endowed with holy properties or spirits known as 'kami'. The Shinto pantheon includes the creator, sun, moon and stars, mountains, rivers, sea and fire, plants and animals. The typical dwelling places of spirits were the hilltop, the crag of rock, and the solitary tree, and in the Shinto shrines rocks and trees are adorned with prayers and ropes of worship, known as 'shimenawa'. Forms which Westerners would consider inanimate have become fused with a vitality through Shinto. Whereas we in the West would mould or break natural form to our own design, the Japanese, recognising the vitality inherent in the form, shape the design to release the vitality. The garden art can capture the movement or flow of nature in forms which we might consider fixed and static.

At the centre of Japanese mythology and Shinto belief is the Sun Goddess, Amaterasu Omikami. She had two brothers, Tsukiyomi, the Moon God, and Susanowo no Mikoto, the Storm God. Amaterasu and Tsukiyomi sat back to back as Sun and Moon in their celestial world, alternating the day and the night. However, Susanowo, the Storm God, was violent and unruly. On one occasion he visited Amaterasu to apologise for previous misdeeds, but instead he set loose wild, piebald colts which ran amok and broke down the walls dividing the rice fields. Then Amaterasu promptly retreated to a cave

and the world was plunged into darkness. The other deities gathered outside the cave, where they planted a sacred tree; on its upper branches they placed a jewel, and in the centre of the tree a mirror. The jewel and the mirror are now two of the sacred treasures of Japan. To the great enjoyment of the assembled deities, a goddess performed a lively and bawdy dance. Amaterasu, inquisitive to discover the source of amusement, peered out of the cave. She then caught her reflection in the mirror and came out into the open, and light was returned to the world.

Ritual is the essence of Shinto practice. The nature of the ritual marks the survival of images rooted in the powers of Sun and Storm. The force of the Storm encounters the power of the Sun. The Storm disrupts the land and the Sun retreats. Only by ritual entreaty does the light of spring return to renew the cycle. The pattern represents the imagery of a primitive agricultural society. The renewal is still celebrated and Amaterasu is enshrined with a ritual of undiminished significance.

The shrine dedicated to the Sun Goddess stands at Ise in Mie Prefecture on the east coast of Honshu. It houses the sacred mirror, which is said to have been brought from the celestial land by Ninigi, the grandson of Amaterasu. The mirror was kept at Yamato, where the ancient rulers of Japan, the priests and tribal chiefs who claimed direct descent from the Sun Goddess, had established their tribal centre. It was then moved to Ise in the first century by the Emperor Suinin (29 B.C.–A.D. 70). From the reign of the Emperor Temmu in the seventh century, the shrine has been pulled down and faithfully reconstructed every twenty years on an immediately adjacent site. It is the holiest shrine in Japan.

Set in a forest clearing, the buildings appear like upturned boats riding on the waves of the forest. The primitive wooden structures merge with the surrounding trees. They are the earliest and finest examples of a pure Japanese architectural style, known as Yu-itsu Shinmei Zukuri, Unique Divine style. Uninfluenced by the Chinese, these are the buildings of a seafaring island race; the parallel with the boat is evident in the structure.

The origins of Japanese architecture lay in the

enclosure of space. The sacred tree was designated and then hung with shimenawa and prayers. The tree was surrounded by a fence and the sanctified space was enclosed. Accordingly the original builders of the shrine of the Sun Goddess defined the space around the shrine with a fence, which established a boundary with the forested wilderness.

The main building is approached along an avenue of tall Japanese cedar (*Cryptomeria japonicum*; Jap. sugi). The shrine is concealed by a high outer fence of wood raised on a stone wall. Behind this is an inner fence of smooth, rounded pillars of bare, unvarnished cedar. The pillars mark the transition from the forest to the enclosed space with a purity and simplicity of form. The inner fence is also rebuilt every twenty years with the main shrine building. It surrounds a large rectangular area, covered with pebbles, in the centre of which stands the shrine itself.

The building rests on pillars, which raise it several feet above the ground. It is crowned with a steeply-sloping roof, with deep overhanging eaves; it has a thick thatch of 'kaya', a miscanthus reed. The line of the curve of the roof is continued in beams, known as 'chigi', at either end of the building, which cross at the apex and protrude up into the sky. Short but heavy beams, 'kat-suogi', are placed horizontally across the ridge of the roof, to give added weight to the thatch to protect it from the high winds of the typhoon. Finest Japanese cypress, hinoki, is used throughout. The joinery of the structure is extremely complex. Nowhere in the entire building are any nails used. There is a strength and solidity beneath the light, floating appearance of the roof. There is an intricate complexity that is so well executed that the building has the quality of simplicity.

The last reconstruction ceremony, Shikinen-Sengu, was completed in 1973. The entire ritual takes place over a period of eight years. It starts with Yamaguchi-sai, a ceremony to honour the God of the Mountain and to pay respect for the thousands of trees that are to be cut for the new shrine. The ritual reaches its climax eight years later when the sacred mirror is installed in the new building. During the most recent enactment of the final ceremony (in 1973), a procession of one hundred and thirty people accompanied the mirror to its new shrine,

terasu is linked to historical fact, and the light of the Sun Goddess is cast over the nation. The legend and others recorded in the Kojiki and the Nihon Shoki, the great chronicles of the eighth century, have been absorbed into Japanese life, instilling a respect for the Emperor which we as Westerners might interpret as excessively nationalistic. Only when seen in the context of mythology is the continued deification of the Emperor conceivable. In more recent history, loyalty to this code of belief has been extreme. The national emotion is volatile and powerful and, like the land itself, from time to time it erupts.

The sacred precincts of the Ise shrine formed the first stage in the development of the garden. The area enclosed by the fence as the site of the shrine, is known as 'yuniwa'. A Japanese word for 'garden' is 'niwa'; it implies a small area of ground. The garden has a peculiar function, for it creates space or an illusion of space. At a time when space has been consumed at an alarming rate to accommodate a dense population and extraordinary industrial expansion, the ability to create space has a particular significance. Japan has been highly populated for centuries. When Western officials visited Japan in the last century, Tokyo was already one of the largest cities in the world. Mountains leave only a small proportion of the total land mass as suitable for habitation. As the landscape has moulded the image, so the space and scale of the land has changed the focus of the imagination.

The walls of the garden, like the fence around the shrine, determine the space. Behind those walls the garden forms its own horizons in a separate world. Within one world is set another, which is a limitless and differently-scaled universe, containing mountain and ocean.

The vitality of this landscape, its violent and subdued extremes, has been ingrained on the Japanese imagination, which has reflected the balance of these extremes. The garden, inseparable from the landscape, guides the eye to realise this balance.

while the Emperor in his palace in Tokyo, two hundred miles to the north, ceremoniously turned and faced the direction of Ise. More than ten thousand worshippers watched the torchlit procession of dignitaries, wearing Shinto costumes from the Heian period, make their way to the new shrine to the accompaniment of music. The sacred mirror is carried in a box within another box, which is wrapped in white silk. No one has the right to see the mirror, except the Emperor, who has never made use of the privilege. The inner of the two boxes is remade every twenty years. By renewing the materials of the shrine and replacing the edifice, the underlying belief is preserved intact.

Amaterasu is the great ancestor of the Japanese Imperial line. Through the Emperor, the legend of Ama-

The Balance of Opposites

Change is a factor that could overwhelm a stranger in Japan. You have to learn to accept the sudden transitions to avoid disorientation. Over the last century change has been swift; during the last twenty years the pace has been unprecedented.

The Japanese city can tangle you in chaos. It sprawls with no plan to its development. Overhead, cables criss-cross above the buildings, neon assaults the senses, the colours jar. A passing train can shake the ground and the hum of traffic absorb its roar. A doorway on the street might lead you into a small courtyard, containing only shrubs and a stone lantern. After this brief pause, on entering the house you are immediately struck by form and order. All around restraint is evident, nothing is superfluous. The uncluttered simplicity of the house yields space. The main room contains little or no furniture. The floor is covered with tatami mats. The colours are quiet, the textures pronounced. The light through the paper screens is soft and diffuse. The absence of glass further seals the detachment from the world outside. There is an ordered harmony, there are no distractions.

There is a Japanese word, 'imamekashi', implying a quality meaning modern or 'up to date'. An object or idea that had 'imamekashi', was relevant to the present situation and was worthy of attention. Attention to past or future was unnecessary. In the light of this focus on the present, the vagueness of much of Japan's early history is understandable. It was easier to relate the image of the myth than the historical fact to the situation of the moment. Unlike the intellectual tradition of the West, the Japanese have no need for speculation or hypothesis on the future, or for digging into the past (it is only since the last World War that archaeology has been widely studied in Japan).

A people whose thoughts are focused on the present live closer to their intuition than their intellect. They experience no abstract linear development from past to present to future, but a cycle of which change is an integral part. When there is no before and no behind, it is conceivable to find serenity in the privacy of the home, even if outside the back door, you have been confronted by visual chaos of nightmare proportions.

The cycle is seen in the orbit of the planets and the return of the season. It reaffirms the healing power of the life force; the renewal of growth after decay. It places life and death on a common continuum. Perpetual motion consumes no energy; the movement always returns the process to an original point. Inherent in this pattern of cyclic motion is a constancy and order. The stability is established by a dynamic relationship between opposite elements, which complement and balance each other. In the same way as it is impossible within this system to isolate past from present, the opposite elements cannot be segregated or the balance is lost. The poles exist only in relation to each other. This interaction is fundamental not only to aesthetics, but to a way of life.

*   *   *

Archaeologists who were investigating a cave on the Muira peninsula, outside Tokyo, in 1973, found the fossilised remains of tortoise-shell lamellae, which they believe to have been used as oracles. Judging by the depth at which the remains were found, and by earthenware shards also discovered in the cave, the lamellae were estimated to be one thousand five hundred years old. They had been scraped from green tortoise-shells, had rectangles carved on their surfaces and revealed cross-shaped burns.

Historical records have for a long time indicated that divination was practised in ancient Japan by means of burning tortoise-shells. A hole was bored in the shell and a burning piece of wood was inserted into it. The cracks, produced by the heat, were interpreted as divine response in the form of a magical writing. The discovery was the first evidence that the practice had been introduced to Japan from China, where it had been widely used during the Shang dynasty in the second millennium B.C. Inscriptions on many of the tortoise-shells which have been excavated from the Shang tombs have verified the details of the practice.

The cosmology of the Chinese in the Archaic period was symbolised in the tortoise. Above, it had a shell which was round like the sky, and below it was considered square like the earth. The image suggested stability; it was perfectly balanced.

The remarkable discovery served as further important evidence to link the ancient civilisation of Japan with that of China. It also illustrated an attitude which is common to both Japanese and Chinese perception of heaven and earth. This attitude is fundamental to Japanese aesthetics and is expressed in activities as diverse as the martial arts, the tea ceremony and the design of the garden.

The tortoise-shell oracle was also of particular significance as the patterns and images used in the practice were later developed in the I Ching, the Book of Changes. It is to the inscriptions on the shells that researchers into the I Ching are now turning. The antithesis of 'above' and 'below' represents a polarity which includes an endless range of relationships. The cardinal concepts of the I Ching are 'Ch'ien' the Creative, and 'K'un' the Receptive. Ch'ien is the father and the ruler, K'un is the mother and the devoted populace. Ch'ien is in the head, K'un is in the abdomen. Ch'ien is red, K'un is black. Ch'ien is the blade, K'un is the cloth. Ch'ien is found as midnight approaches, K'un is in the afternoon sun. The season of Ch'ien is the oncoming of winter, that of K'un is the full maturity of late summer.

An archetypal vision of the universe, expressed in the language of diviners in the second millennium B.C., became crystallised in the images of the Creative, above, and the Receptive, below. Rather than fixed points, these were active, moving forces, alternating with the cycle of events. These forces encompassed the farthest reaches of the imagination of men living in the most direct contact with the elements—the cave-dwellers of prehistory. The sum of their experience could be contained in the interaction between Ch'ien and K'un.

In the path of these concepts a pattern was established, which could be observed in the motion of planets and which can be seen today in the microstructure of matter. If the two characteristics were considered as different aspects of a common force or movement, one quality could not be achieved by denial of the other. Only if the balance between the two characteristics was understood, would one quality become apparent by its own nature.

In an aesthetic context, obviously beauty was pleasing to the Japanese sensibility and ugliness was not. As soon as the striving for beauty was self-conscious, forced or pretentious, then beauty was lost. Beauty flourished where there was least desire to create it—in the accidents of Nature. The tea masters of the Muromachi period fully understood this principle and further developed it in their appreciation of the simple, uncontrived quality of the rough folk-wares of the rural craftsmen. The role of the artist was to act as the agent through which beauty took form, not as a creator or controller extracting beauty. Such a role required recognition of the delicacy of the balance.

The extent to which the balance was applied is well illustrated in the art of swordsmanship. The practice of the art involves an extreme pitch of alertness. There is no room for superfluous thinking—the senses must be acutely sharpened. To falter in a moment of fear would be the cause of one's destruction. Through his discipline the master understands the indiscerptibility of life and death, as opposite coordinates of the same cycle. He has no time to think of strategy of defence and strategy of attack—his movements become so fast that they are one continuous motion. He will realise that he will win when he has merged himself into one with his opponent.

I sometimes feel that when the marionette master puts his mind wholly into the play, his state of mind attains something of the swordsman's. He is then not conscious of the distinction between himself and the doll he manipulates. The play becomes really an art when the master enters into a state of emptiness. Some may feel like seeing a difference between the marionette master and the swordsman, because of the latter's confrontation with a living personality who is aiming every moment at striking you down. But my way of thinking is different, in as much as both have realised the state of identity, it must operate alike regardless of its objectives.

When the identity is realised, I as swordsman see no opponent confronting me and threatening to strike me. I seem to transform myself into the opponent, and every movement he makes, as well as every thought he conceives are felt as if they were all my own and I intuitively, or rather

[19]

unconsciously know when and how to strike him. All seems to be so natural.

Takano Shigeyoshi*

The art of swordsmanship personified the integration of opposites. The ability to project yourself into the being of your opponent, until the identification was complete—until you became that opponent, lies close to the spirit which is the essence of Zen. However, if Zen was conceptualised as a development of a principle expressed in Chinese thought, as found in the I Ching, or if it was argued that its origins lay in a dynamic relationship between opposite elements, the very power of Zen would be denied. It has been stated that the more you talk about Zen the more blatantly you have misunderstood it. To define Zen would be to deny it.

To our logical Western minds, which long to grasp firm and absolute concepts, this may seem most mysterious. But let it suffice for now that the attitude, which is so fundamental to Japanese aesthetics, is found in the spirit of Zen as Zen pervaded the culture of Japan. If both the animate and inanimate forms of nature were experienced as a life force, then to approach a point of identification with the landscape, which we might describe as harmony, is as conceivable as to coalesce yourself with a physical opponent. It is through the garden that we can understand that identification and it is there that the subtleties of Zen can be stripped of their mystery and can be directly suggested.

★　　　★　　　★

Geomancy, a sacred science of land surveyance and divination, has been practised in China certainly as recently as the late nineteenth century. The practice was called Feng Shui, which meant 'wind and water', because it was as intangible as the wind and like water it was impossible to grasp. On several occasions in the mid-nineteenth century, British merchants were obstructed from executing their building and development schemes on account of the obscure Feng Shui. A gov-

ernor of Macao, Senor Amaral, who is said to have had little respect for Feng Shui and a great enthusiasm for building roads, was even attacked and decapitated in revenge for his disregard for the principles of geomancy.

A geomancer was consulted when the site of an important building or tomb was to be located. He attributed the male and female characteristics, yang and yin, to the landscape and detected a positive, yang current of energy, which ran through sharp, jagged mountain forms, and a negative, yin current in soft, gently undulating hill country. The yang current was symbolised in the azure dragon and the yin current in the white tiger. The point where the dragon met the tiger would be the most auspicious site for the building. Land where neither currents were evident, such as on a great plain, would be considered unsuitable.

With the aid of a compass, and by observing the direction of flow of a river or stream in the vicinity, the geomancer determined the point where the two qualities were balanced. At such a place, the pattern of the celestial forces of the planets would be considered appropriately balanced and reflected in the harmony of the landscape. The contrasting forms of the land at that particular point would contain a boundless image of the forces of Nature. Obviously, to the Chinese the laying of roads across the paths of the dragon and tiger forces did more than disrupt the scenery—it cut the flow of vital currents.

The geomantic tradition is evident in the design of the garden. The Secret Books on gardening, which were published in Japan during the Tokugawa period, contained old texts on design and details of technique. The geomantic principles described in the books were interpreted as fixed and rigid rules and such an interpretation greatly contributed to a decline in the garden art. However, like the Chinese geomancer, the gardener looked for a scene in which the huge scope of Nature could be expressed—where mountains, forests, oceans and rivers could be seen in stone and sand, moss and pools.

According to the Secret Books, the garden was laid out in relation to the cardinal points of the compass. The direction of flow of the stream through the garden was

---

* Takano Shigeyoshi: 1958. One of the greatest swordsmen of modern Japan. See D. T. Suzuki: *Zen and Japanese Culture*.

also important, though there appears to have been some confusion over this point. Some authorities said that the flow should be from east to west, a stream running from west to east being very unlucky; other sources thought that the flow should be in the opposite direction. Importance was likewise attached to the points of entrance and exit of the stream into and from the garden. The position of pavilions in the grounds of large gardens would be subject to the same geomantic principles.

Application of these principles encouraged a balance in the general features of the composition. However, it is probable that a balance obtained by pure intuition would conform to a balance prescribed by the principles. The importance of intuition in the composition cannot be overemphasised. The geomantic principles provided no more than a framework or context within which the design could be developed, and they stressed that a universal harmony could be expressed in a miniature image of that balance. Strict adherence to any rule of design was contrary to the spontaneous spirit with which so much of the garden art was practised.

The balance was extended to details of the design by contrast in the shape, size and colour of the garden forms. As according to Shinto belief, trees, rocks, mountains and springs are endowed with gender, so too are the rocks and trees in the garden attributed with male and female characteristics. Often there would be principal male and female stones; the male stone would be placed in an exposed situation, whereas the female stone would lie in a shaded and more secluded spot. Strong, upright forms were considered masculine and low, round forms were feminine.

Great care would be taken in the selection of the appropriate combination of the opposite forms. A combination that offended sensibility, demonstrated an imbalance that was most inauspicious; it would betray not only aesthetic taste but also the harmonious order of Nature. The tall, straight form of a male stone would be emphasised by an adjacent female stone. The full potential of a form was realised through its relation to its opposite.

To be true to the landscape, the natural laws were faithfully observed in the garden. Flowers, shrubs and trees were planted in situations that corresponded with their natural habitat. Overcrowded displays of rare plants or collections of unusual stones would be considered not only ostentatious or incongruous but impure. A specific choice of flowers, a particular style of bridge or a clump of trees might suggest a particular beauty spot or view on which the garden was modelled. However, garden designers avoided following the details of a real landscape too closely lest the results appeared contrived. The garden was extended far beyond the reproduction of natural views; the skill of the designer was in suggestion not representation, in restraint not explicitness.

That beauty and ugliness were one and part of the same perception has already been implied. Accordingly, absolute perfection, in which no trace of the imperfect was found, would fail to embody beauty. It was through imperfection that perfection was recognised and beauty appreciated. A form that was perfect would be static and dead. This feeling was realised by the tea masters who delighted in the asymmetrical forms of the tea room and the stepping-stones of the tea garden, or in the choice of the irregularly-shaped utensils.

Likewise, the architecture of the Buddhist temple followed no geometrical pattern in Japan, for though the main hall and the main gate of the temple may have been built on a central axis, the adjoining buildings of the complex were not positioned to satisfy symmetry but to merge into the contours of the landscape. The balance was not geometrical but followed natural features. The rhythm of the building became the rhythm of its background.

The relationship between garden and building was important. Like the temple the Japanese house is not compact (the architecture of the Zen temple is based on domestic architecture); it is divided into separate wings, connected by covered passages and verandahs, which link garden and house. The garden both surrounds the building and lies within it. The garden can become an extension of the building.

Solemn, impressive and graceful—symmetry is the manifestation of a logical, calculating intellect. The Japanese had no need for the creation of a new abstract order. They intuitively found their identity in the balance of the landscape and the passing of the season. Throughout the garden the asymmetrical patterns of bridges, paths, stones and trees retain the impression that there is no design at all. The garden becomes the accident of Nature.

The Islands and the Mainland

The modern Japanese city cannot be equated with urban development elsewhere in the world. There is nothing unfamiliar in the exterior, superficial façade of the centre of Tokyo. Office blocks rise in the business area of the city, much like offices anywhere. Shop windows display the same consumer goods as are seen in the shops of western Europe or the United States, though there are obvious specialisations. Apart from the blatant difference of the oriental features of the passers-by, the written characters of the shop signs and the strange smells of a new city, there is a somewhat intangible distinction between the Japanese city with its post-war Western exteriors and a modern European capital.

The symptoms of city life are more extreme; the crowds are that much thicker, the traffic heavier, the pace faster, the air dirtier and the wealth more defined. The real standard of living is lower than most European cities despite the apparent prosperity. The space to spread yourself, to move unrestricted, the sympathy of the individual with the actual architecture and fabric of the city, the sense of identity with the man beside you on the street, are all features which are noticeably absent. It is a parody of the modern Western city and all its faults.

If you enter through the impressive doors of a typical Japanese company office, past the machinery of business, the secretaries, typewriters and computers, you are likely to find the businessman rapidly calculating on his abacus. The exterior of the institution is Western, but behind the closed doors the heart of the business is conducted in a typically Japanese fashion. Likewise, the modern city, with all its pretensions of Westernisation, remains peculiarly Japanese. This strange, multi-layered environment has been described in the very precise image of a rod: the outer wrapping of the rod is of cellophane—representing the superficial, transparent exterior beneath which is a rod of steel—the strength of modern, industrial Japan; enclosed within the steel is a length of bamboo—the true strength of Japan, at the centre of which is emptiness or the void.

In accordance with their insular tradition, the Japanese have never allowed themselves to be wholly swallowed up by foreign influences. A very significant pattern can be seen in the process of Westernisation. It is a sequence of imitation, absorption and then reinterpretation. The same pattern can be seen in the earlier history and previous influences on these island people, in particular in the influence of the great civilisation of the mainland of China. It was from China that the first influences on garden design came in the sixth century. It was again from China that there came influences of a different kind, which in the nineteenth century were to lead to a decline in the garden art.

Communication between Japan and China had existed from as early as the first century A.D. The Empress Jingo is said to have led a military expedition to Korea in the middle of the fourth century, probably after a series of raids across the Korean straits. A Japanese colony was then established on the tip of the Korean peninsula and an important link was formed with the mainland of the continent. The Muira oracle discovery provides direct evidence of Chinese cultural influence on Japan in the fourth or fifth century. The significance of the tortoise-shell oracle as a rudimentary foundation for the I Ching, and its subsequent influence on the thought of China and Japan cannot be underestimated.

Also of great importance was the official introduction of the Chinese script at the start of the fifth century, even though at the time it was used by only a small group of scholars and scribes. Korean settlers arrived in Japan bringing with them skilled metal workers and the knowledge of sericulture. One hundred thousand Koreans and Manchurians were resident by the middle of the sixth century. A flood of new ideas from the great Chinese empire was to reach Japan via Korea. The doors to the unprecedented brilliance of the T'ang dynasty were opened. Together with the technical skills and fresh artistic imagination, came the continental religion, Buddhism. In A.D. 552 the Emperor Syöng-Möng (Seimei) of Pekche (Kudara) in south-west Korea sent a mission to the court of the Japanese Emperor Kimmei to strengthen an alliance.

According to the Nihon Shoki, the mission presented the Japanese Emperor with a gilded, bronze statue of the Buddha Sakyamuni and several sutras (Buddhist texts). The arrival of this mission marks the official introduction of Buddhism to Japan, and also the start of the great flow of ideas from the continent. Throughout

the reign of the Empress Suiko, close contact with Korea and then China was greatly encouraged under the regency of Prince Shotoku. Japanese diplomats and scholars travelled to the continent, eager to seal diplomatic relations, also characteristically to acquire knowledge of the magnificent civilisation and to study the sutras.

The travellers, statesmen, scholars and artists from Japan, who made the voyage down the Inland Sea then across the straits of Korea, were doubtless impressed by the coastline and the islands of their own country. The journey, in addition to widening their previously very limited horizons, would have given them a new perspective on Japan itself. On their return, many of the travellers described the coasts of their native land. The fresh stimulus of these experiences was reflected in the garden in its early, primitive stage; the new sources of inspiration were evident.

In the tumulus periods from the fourth to the sixth centuries, the empty, gravelled courtyard of the Imperial Palace was called 'yuniwa' when used for Shinto rituals and 'oniwa' when used for official State functions ('niwa' meaning garden or space; see Ch. 1). A part of the secular 'oniwa' was made into a lake. The pebbled edge of the lake was called 'suhana', meaning a gravelled seashore, and the banks, which were bordered with larger stones, were called 'ariso', meaning a rocky beach. Significantly, however, from the middle of the sixth century until the eighth century, another word, 'shima', was used to mean garden. At that time the word 'shima' also had the same meaning as it has today—it means 'island'.

The early Japanese gardens therefore were subject to several influences, as a result of the contact established with the main continent. As well as a new imaginative conception of the landscape of Japan itself, there were the splendours of the T'ang dynasty and its artistic vigour, the Imperial gardens of China and practical lessons in garden design, and lastly the most important cultural vehicle, Buddhism.

A very exotic fantasy of the Chinese garden was developed in the West as a result of the descriptions of the early European travellers in the Orient. Sir William Chambers, an eighteenth-century traveller and architect, left a remarkable account of Chinese gardening, which he claimed he wrote as a result of conversations with Chinese artists and from his own observations in China.

The Chinese, in their large gardens, contrive different scenes for different times of day, disposing at the points of view buildings which from their use point out the proper hour for enjoying the view in its perfections. They have besides scenes for every season of the year: some for winter, generally exposed to the southern sun, and composed of pines, firs and cedars, evergreen oaks, phillyreas, hollies, yews and many other evergreens, being enriched with laurels of various sorts, laurestinus, arbutus, and other plants; and to give variety and gaiety to these gloomy productions, they plant among them in regular forms, divided by walks, all the rare shrubs, flowers, and trees of the torrid zone, which they cover during the winter with frames of glass disposed in the form of temples and other elegant buildings. Their scenes of spring likewise abound with evergreens, intermixed with lilacs of all sorts, laburnums, limes, larixes, double-blossomed thorn, almond and peach trees; with sweet brier, early rose and honeysuckle. The ground and verges of the thickets and shrubberies are adorned with wild hyacinths, wall flowers, daffodils, violets, primroses, polyanthus, crocuses, daisies, snowdrops and various species of iris. . . . Their summer scenes compose the richest and most studied parts of their gardens. They abound with lakes, rivers, and water works of every contrivance, and with vessels of every construction, . . . The woods consist of oak, beech, Indian chestnut, elm, ash, plane, sycamore, maple, arbutus, and several other species of the poplar, with many other trees peculiar to China. The thickets are composed of every deciduous plant that grows in the climate, and every flower or shrub that flourishes during the summer months; all uniting to form the finest verdure, and most brilliant, harmonious colouring imaginable.★

The description continues with such images that can be afforded only by poetic licence. However, the account does provide valuable botanical information and illustrates the fundamental distinction of the Oriental garden from the ancient Egyptian, Persian and Mediterranean gardens; the emphasis of the design is on

★ See Josiah Conder: *Landscape Gardening in Japan.*

[25]

conformity to the laws of Nature rather than to the laws of symmetry or geometry. The various scenes, which contain a vast range of trees, shrubs and flowering plants appropriate to each season, and the abounding lakes and rivers, indicate an intention to create a world in the garden as natural as the wild landscape that was its inspiration.

The scale of these large Chinese parks must have been enormous; certainly large enough to encompass the scenes described by Chambers. For the Sea and Mountain Records of Sui Yang Ti (Sui Yang Ti Hai Shan Chi) record that in the year A.D. 607 the Emperor Sui Yang Ti was building a park near his capital Lo-Yang,

To create his Western Park, the ground was broken over an area two hundred li in circuit (about seventy-five miles) and the labour of a million workers was required. Within the park were constructed sixteen courts (residential palaces built around interior courtyards). Earth and rock were brought to make hills and the ground was excavated for the Five Lakes and the Four Seas (the Northern Sea had a perimeter of thirteen miles). . . . A proclamation was issued directing all those in the vicinity (of the capital) possessing plants, trees, birds, and beasts, should dispatch them to the park. From everywhere, then, were collected innumerable quantities of flowers, herbs, plants, trees, birds, beasts, fishes and frogs, and even these were not fully sufficient.

This immense landscape work would certainly have been observed by Japanese visitors to the Sui capital, and it could hardly have failed to have been impressive. The Western Park of Sui Yang Ti was not an isolated monumental labour, for the tradition of the huge landscape parks was continued. Marco Polo, writing in the twelfth century of the court of Kublai Khan, gives this description of the grounds of the Khan's palace,

In the north-western corner of the grounds is a pit of great size and depth, very neatly made, from which the earth was removed to build the mound of which I shall speak. The pit is filled with water by a fair sized stream so as to form a sort of pond where the animals come to drink. . . . On the northern side of the palace at the distance of a bow shot but still within the walls, the Great Khan has made an earthwork, that is to say a mound fully one hundred paces in height and over a mile in circumference. This mound is covered with a dense growth of trees, all evergreens that never shed their leaves. And I assure you that whenever the Great Khan hears tell of a particularly fine tree, he has it pulled up, roots and all and with a quantity of earth, and transported to this mound by elephants. No matter how big the tree may be, he is not deterred from transplanting it.

The artificial mountain, formed from the excavation of the lake, can still be seen in Peking, in the Park of Sea Palaces, the last of the Imperial Parks. It is an island in what is known as the Northern Sea, Pei Hai. On its slopes there is still a juniper, which is thought to have survived from the Khan's magnificent arboretum. Like the park of Sui Yang Ti, the Park of Sea Palaces was once called the Western Park (it lies to the west of the Winter Palace in the Forbidden City), and though its scale is not as vast as the earlier park, its style is very similar. It was an obvious model for the Japanese garden, as is evident when one examines the revival of Chinese influence during the Tokugawa period. Despite its extensive area, the Park of Sea Palaces lies within the walls of the Forbidden City, so further emphasising the barrier between the common horizons of the people and the separate world of the garden, in this case secluded for the privilege of the court.

There was a strong relationship between the construction of such landscapes and landscape painting. The gardener and the landscape painter expressed a common image. Throughout the development of landscape painting, which was to reach a peak in Japan in the fifteenth century, there can be seen the concurrent development of the garden design. Some of the greatest Japanese gardeners were also painters.

In China, during the Period of Six Dynasties (Liu Tai, A.D. 317–589), the style of painting which was previously almost entirely figurative began to include landscape painting. One of the most famous landscape painters of the period, Tsung Ping (A.D. 375–443), wrote a *Preface to Painting*, a treatise on landscape. This has been translated, and in places interpreted rather than literally translated by Alexander Soper.

'Landscapes have a material existence, and yet reach into

* Quotations appearing on pp. 26 and 27, see Lorraine Kuck: *The World of the Japanese Garden.*

[26]

a spiritual domain.' The wild beauty of their forms, the 'peaks and precipices rising sheer and high, the cloudy forest lying dense and vast', have brought to the wise and virtuous recluses of the past an unending pleasure, a 'joy which is of the soul, and of the soul only'. One approach to the Tao is by inward concentration alone; another almost the same, is through the beauty of mountains and water. 'In such a way the beauty of Mount Sung and Mount Hua, the very mystery of the Dark Spirit of the Universe, all may be captured within a single picture.'★

It is clear that contemplation and a profound awareness of landscape meant more than pleasing aesthetics— it was the path to spiritual enlightenment, the Tao. The mystery of that path could also be expressed, or as Tsung Ping said, 'captured' in a single scene. A comparison with the aims of the gardener is very relevant, for one of the terms of Japanese garden design is 'shakkei', which had the original literal meaning, 'a landscape captured alive'. That same mystery could be captured in the garden.

Two examples of Japanese pictorial art of the early seventh century, that are still in existence at Horyu-ji, near Nara, indicate that the early Buddhist art of Japan reflected the archaic style of the Six Dynasties. This reached Japan via Korea about one hundred years after it had originated in China. Both works of art, the painted panels at the base of the Shaka-Nyorai (Sakyamuni) statue (A.D. 623), and the pair of large embroideries, the Tenjukoku Mandala at Chugu-ji, Nara, depict landscapes. They are the landscapes of the Gods— the images of paradise. The landscape was fused with the religious ideal.

The Nihon Shoki records that in A.D. 612 a man named Roshi no Takumi, who was also known as Shikomaro, 'the ugly artisan', arrived in Japan from Paekshe in Korea. Apparently he was disfigured by a blotchy skin, which the Japanese found distasteful. They wanted to banish him as a castaway on an island. He is said to have replied,

If you dislike my spotted skin, you should not breed cattle and horses that are spotted with white. Moreover, I have a small talent. I can make the figures of hills and mountains. If you keep me and make use of me, it would be to the ad-

vantage of the country. Why should you waste me by casting me away on an island in the sea?★

In the southern courtyard or 'oniwa' of the palace of the Empress Suiko he did indeed build a Chinese bridge and a replica of Mount Shumisen (Sumeru). This mountain features in the Buddhist cosmology as the highest peak in the world, reaching up to the heavens, and the core of the universe. It is often symbolised in the garden by a large rock. The particular Mount Shumisen built by Roshi no Takumi represents the starting point of the Japanese rock garden, and marks the first use of stone to depict mountains.

In 1903 a stone image, which is believed to be a 'Shumisen' dating from the reign of the Empress Suiko, was excavated at Asuka, near Nara. It consists of three levels of granite carved to fit together to form a monument about eight feet high; it is thought that a fourth layer once existed. The surface of the stone is carved with wave-like lines, which suggest a mountain range. The stones are hollow, and there is an opening in the top stone through which water could flow to several openings in the bottom stone, which would thus form a fountain.

The site of the excavation on the river bank east of Amakashi Hill was believed to be that of the garden of a famous government minister of the sixth century, Soga no Umako. The Nihon Shoki records that there was a lake and an island in his garden, after which Umako was known as 'the Lord of the Island'. To warrant such a title, one can suppose that the garden must have been very impressive. Judging by the grave of Soga no Umako, the 'stone stage grave mound' at Asuka, he must have had considerable status. All the earth on the burial mound has been washed away to leave just the entrance passage and the massive stone structure of the burial chamber. Umako would not only have had a sufficient labour force to construct a large garden, but those who laboured for their master were evidently highly skilled at working with stone.

Other replicas of Mount Shumisen were erected in A.D. 657 to the west of Asuka temple and in A.D. 660 at the end of Isonokami pond. The Empress Saimei (who reigned A.D. 655–661) also followed the garden

of voyages down the Inland Sea, across the Straits of Korea and the Sea of Japan, and also from the influence of the great lakes and islands of the huge Chinese landscape parks. The image of the mountain, however, comes directly from the thrusting volcanic forms of the Japanese landscape. It was the mountain, reaching into the heaven above the clouds, that contained the very mystery of the 'Dark Spirit of the Universe'. With the spread of Buddhism, the symbol of Mount Shumisen channelled this mystery into orthodox cosmology.

Buddhism was of social and political significance as it was a vehicle of artistic and cultural significance. The idea of a unified religion under central, national control conformed to the plan of a centralised, bureaucratic machinery of government modelled after the Chinese system. Buddhist texts, such as the Ninno-Kyo, the sutra of Benevolent Kings, emphasised this mood of national unity in the late seventh century. The concentration of power after economic and administrative reform in A.D. 645 led to closer contact with China. Instead of the gradual spread of Chinese artistic achievements down the Korean peninsula and so to Japan, the splendours of T'ang art and T'ang poetry were readily absorbed by the still closer contact with the mainland, which was obtained as a result of this centralisation. The architecture, sculpture and painting of the seventh century are evidence of the great rise to artistic maturity, stimulated by the wide scope of ideas received from China.

style of creating artificial mountains. In A.D. 689 the death of Prince Kusakabe was commemorated in twenty mournful poems, among which is a description of his garden at his palace at Asuka. The description mentions a 'fragrant pool' containing water fowl and the banks of which had areas of 'suhana' (gravelled seashore) and 'ariso' (rocky beach). There was an island that could be reached by a Chinese bridge and a footpath followed the shoreline, along which were planted azaleas.

Even within these brief and limited accounts of the early gardens, important details were revealed, on which garden designs were later based. The rudimentary features were established. The images of the seascape and the islands were derived from the experiences

Until the eighth century, there had been no cities or towns in Japan. In the past (according to Shinto custom) on the death of the Emperor, the capital was moved for fear of pollution. It was necessary to establish a permanent seat of government. A new capital was built at Nara in A.D. 710, which was modelled on the T'ang capital, Chang'an. The city of Nara covered an area of about seven and a half square miles, a quarter of the size of its model. It was rectangular in shape and lined with broad, straight thoroughfares. Unlike Chang'an it had no city walls and the western half of the city was never completed. However, the city of Nara, together with the earlier temple of Horyu-ji (seventh century), contain the finest examples of architecture in the T'ang style to be found anywhere—the oldest wooden buildings in the world.

The construction of the city marked the culminating stage in the absorption of Chinese influences. The city would have been of extraordinary beauty, judging by the superb temple architecture that remains. Both the exterior of the city and its institutions were borrowed from China. A foreign culture had been imitated with enthusiasm and very rapidly assimilated. But, despite the overwhelming Chinese influence, native traditions were still preserved. Buddhism did not replace Shinto. With typical Japanese ingenuity, the Shinto gods were incorporated into the Buddhist pantheon, and became Bodhisattvas; the two religions were not mutually exclusive and were practised side by side. Beneath the Chinese façade, the Japanese identity was never lost.

Little is known of the gardens of Nara. The nobility built their residences in Chinese style and there are records of lake gardens in the city; one was built by Tachibana no Moroe in A.D. 757 and another by Nakaomi no Kiyomaro in A.D. 758. One can assume that the gardens contained features found in the Asuka gardens. But in addition to the elegant mansions of the aristocracy, there was another less conspicuous development, which contains a clue as to why certain features of the Chinese culture were assimilated so readily. On the outskirts of the city, the noblemen built small rustic retreats like country cottages. The Manyoshu contains poems written by the Emperor Shomu and the Empress Gensho after a visit to such a retreat belonging to Prince Nagaya at Saho.

There was a basic affinity between the Japanese and the Chinese, which was rooted in their great sympathy for Nature. The simple, contemplative life, stripped of superficial clutter and the elaborate refinement of life in the city, was suggested with an unsentimental, penetrating beauty by the T'ang poets. One particular poet, Han-Shan, exemplified this detachment. He lived as a hermit on a mountain-side near T'ien-T'ai.

He looked like a tramp. His body and face were old and beat. Yet in every word he breathed was a meaning in line with subtle principles of things, if only you thought of it deeply. Everything he said had a feeling of the Tao in it, profound and arcane secrets. His hat was made of birch bark, his clothes were ragged and worn out, and his shoes were wood. Thus men who have made it hide their tracks: unifying categories and interpenetrating things.

Lu Ch'iu-Yin, Governor of T'ai Prefecture

His poems were written on the walls of cliffs, on rocks and trees; they were in the colloquial T'ang, direct and uncomplicated, born out of experience, not romanticised beauty. Han-Shan called Cold Mountain his home, but it is more than that—Han-Shan is Cold Mountain. The road to Cold Mountain was his path to enlightenment.

Men ask the way to Cold Mountain
Cold Mountain: there's no through trail.
In summer, ice doesn't melt
The rising sun blurs in swirling fog.
How did I make it?
My heart's not the same as yours.
If your heart was like mine
You'd get it and be right here.

Clambering up the Cold Mountain path,
The Cold Mountain trail goes on and on:
The long gorge choked with scree and boulders,
The wide creek, the mist-blurred grass.
The moss is slippery, though there's been no rain
The pine sings, but there's no wind.
Who can leap the world's ties
And sit with me among the white clouds?

Cold Mountain is a house
Without beams or walls.
The six doors left and right are open
The hall is blue sky.
The rooms all vacant and vague
The east wall beats on the west wall
At the centre nothing.

If I hide out at Cold Mountain
Living off mountain plants and berries—
All my lifetime, why worry?
One follows his karma through.
Days and months slip by like water.
Time is like sparks knocked off flint.

Go ahead and let the world change—
I'm happy to sit among these cliffs.

My home was Cold Mountain from the start,
Rambling among the hills, far from trouble.
Gone, and a million things leave no trace
Loosed, and it flows through the galaxies
A fountain of light, into the very mind—
Not a thing, and yet it appears before me:
Now I know the pearl of the Buddha-nature
Know its use: a boundless perfect sphere.

A serene fulfilment was found in solitude, and in the purity of living high on the mountain, touching the clouds. Among the moss-covered crags and clear streams there was a tranquillity born out of a direct communion with Nature. Such qualities as purity and tranquillity lie close to the spirit of Zen. The figure of the hermit Han-Shan, under his Japanese title Kanzan, was later to be frequently depicted by the Zen painters. Of all the lessons that were assimilated from China, none would have been more readily accepted by the Japanese than this sense of identity with the world of Nature.

The recurring image of Japan as an island rising steeply out of the ocean constantly reaffirms that separate Japanese identity. The geographical insularity and social seclusion of Japan over relatively long periods of the country's development, in effect ensured the survival of a world completely alien and strangely fascinating to the West. One can only speculate on how much longer that world might survive.

The gardener repeated the image of the island in the rock, or the mountain in perfect balance against the 'sea' of the garden.

The Garden of Dreams

In the year A.D. 784, only seventy-five years after the founding of the city of Heijo (Nara), the capital was transferred to Nagoaka. The reasons for the sudden move are unknown. After less than a decade, the capital was changed yet again, this time to a site only ten miles to the north. This second site was more auspiciously situated. Hills lay to the east, west and north, and to the north-east, traditionally the unlucky direction, was Mount Hiei where a great Buddhist monastery and temples had been established, so protecting the city from evil forces. The Kamo river flowed from the east to the south of the site, and the Katsura river flowed on the west.

There was ample water for a city—canals were to run down many of the streets, and there was also sufficient supply for the construction of artificial streams in the gardens. The city was sometimes referred to as the City of Purple Hills and Crystal Streams; the combination of the yang currents of the mountains and the yin forces of the rivers, were perfectly balanced in accordance with the principles of Feng Shui. The cost and labour involved in the transfer of the capital would have been enormous. To repeat the move after less than ten years, for the sake of a finer balance in the natural currents, is indicative of the strength of the geomantic tradition.

The new capital was called Heian Kyo, City of Peace and Tranquillity. The name cleverly combined the first syllable of Heijo, the previous capital, and the last syllable of Chang'an, its model. Like Heijo, the plan of the new city was copied from the great T'ang capital. It covered a rectangular area of about ten and a half square miles,* which was larger than Heijo. A regular, chequer-board pattern was planned with parallel streets and broad avenues, which crossed at right angles, between evenly-spaced intervals. This symmetry was not to be repeated in subsequent urban development. The Suzaku Oji, Red Bird Avenue, which ran from north to south through the centre of the city, was nearly three hundred feet wide.† The great tree-lined avenue, like its model

* The area of Chang'an was thirty square miles and the population greater than one million. Reischauer and Fairbank: *East Asia: The Great Tradition.*

† In Rome, the Twelve Tables prescribed a maximum width of fifteen feet for the 'viae'. The Appian Way was less than twenty feet wide. See I. Morris: *The World of the Shining Prince.*

in Chang'an (which had the staggering width of six hundred feet), was named after the red phoenix, the Chinese symbol for the south—a symbol rooted in geomancy.

The city is known now as Kyoto. It served as the Imperial capital of Japan for more than a thousand years. Until the twelfth century it was the site of an extraordinary era in Japanese history. It was a period when the focus of the Japanese shifted from the outward, acquisitive and imitative characteristics of the preceding phase to become more introspective and even more fervently insular. The result was a world of dazzling, unsurpassed elegance, combined with an understanding and appreciation of the quality of simplicity. Like any aristocratic society, the world of the court was divorced from the grim, barbaric reality of the peasant population. The city of Heian Kyo flourished in complete isolation from the productive sources of the nation. Rising like the lotus flower from the slime, its bloom was magnificent, but due to that very isolation which had nurtured such beauty, the glory could not be sustained.

At the centre of the city stood the Imperial Palace, Kokyo. The buildings have been destroyed by fire on several occasions, and the site transferred. The style of the buildings has changed according to contemporary influences or the prosperity of the Imperial family. A reconstruction of the original Heian palace, based on existing records such as the twelfth-century Nenju-gyoji picture scroll, was completed in 1790; this too was destroyed by fire in 1854. The present buildings date from a repeated reconstruction the following year. They do, however, clearly illustrate how beneath the predominant Chinese influence on the Heian architecture, another style emerges, which is born out of a strong Japanese tradition.

This is evident in simplicity, reminiscent of the earliest Japanese architecture—that of the shrine at Ise— and a sense of space, which is firmly linked to the space of the bare, sanctified courtyard of the shrine, the yuniwa. The residence of the Emperor, a deity, did indeed reflect the atmosphere of a shrine. The man at the summit of such a pronounced social hierarchy, with a magnificent court unparalleled in Japanese history, in an isolated world of splendid ritual, familiar with the

[31]

wonders of T'ang China, instilled in his immediate surroundings the simplicity and comparative austerity of his native, Shinto tradition.

The largest building in the palace complex is the Shishinden, the ceremonial audience hall, which was used for such state functions as the enthronement of the Emperor or the formal New Year audience. Its name was probably borrowed from the hall erected in Chang-'an in A.D. 662. The building faces south. The sweeping curve of its roof is in T'ang style, but instead of heavy tiles, it is covered with the shingled bark of Japanese cypress, hinoki. The roof is supported by wooden pillars so characteristic of Japanese architecture. Within, there are paintings which have been executed on to sliding screens, not directly on to the walls as at Chang'an. An elevated wooden floor spreads out on to a verandah. A wide wooden staircase leads down to the great space of the rectangular, enclosed courtyard. If the building had been erected in true Chinese style, the floors would have been of stone.

Though the curve of the roof was Chinese, the foundations were distinctly Japanese. The walls of the courtyard consist of a corridor with a tiled roof, supported on painted vermilion pillars. Adjacent to the corridor, beneath the eaves of the tiled roof, is a trough of running water. To the east of the steps of the hall stands a cherry tree, Sakon-no-Sakura, and to the west a mandarin orange tree, Ukon-no-Tachibana; the names Sakon and Ukon were derived from the offices of the archers and horsemen stationed at these positions. The courtyard, bare except for these two trees, is an open expanse of raked white sand. One can walk around the courtyard, but never step on to it, let alone traverse it—it is an inviolable image that spreads like a calm ocean.

Next to the Shishinden is the Seiryoden, the Serene and Cool Chamber, which has a stream running beneath its steps. The building faces east and west, so minimising the heat. In front of the western verandah is a small courtyard covered with white sand and clumps of bush clover. This is the bush-clover garden, hagi tsubo, the simplest of all garden compositions. The surface of the garden is flat, there are no stones, no moss and no water. The choice of a single variety of the bush

clover, a most common, inconspicuous plant, is modest. This understatement, the opposite of vulgar ostentation, is executed with a spirit with which the Japanese are most sympathetic. After the plants have flowered in the autumn, they are cut back and the following spring they start to bud again. In the absence of any other features, this the fundamental garden activity, the flowering, the cutting back, the regrowth, becomes the most conspicuous element of the garden. It is the essential element of change.

Through this garden one can see the difference between the Japanese approach to expression and a Western attitude. In the West we tend to 'build up' a picture by a process of addition; starting from a bare framework, we add further details until the picture is complete. The Japanese approach is one of reduction, of stripping back the superfluous layers until the raw image is revealed. That is not to say that the details are insignificant, but when the unnecessary is removed and the elaborate elements reduced, then the details are brought into clearer focus. This is a process of simplification, in the light of which one can see why the quality of purity was so highly regarded in Japan. The process takes one closer to the essence, the real matter of things. The process of reduction is also the process of creation of space. One exceptional Westerner who clearly experienced such a process and knew something of the dynamics of space, the sculptor and painter Alberto Giacometti, said,

I do not believe in the problem of space; space is created solely by the objects; an object that moves without any relation to another object could not give the impression of space. The subject alone is decisive, space, shapes, canvas, plaster, bronze ... so many means. The only important thing is to create a new object, which conveys an impression as close as possible to that received when contemplating the subject. ... Sculpture rests in the void. One *hollows out* space so as to construct the object, and the object as such creates space, the space that exists between the subject and the sculptor.
Conversation between André Parinaud and Alberto Giacometti. *Arts* Nv.873, June 1962

Before the steps in the front courtyard of the Seiryoden stand two ornamental bamboos in trellised enclosures. The presence of these two trees, as in the Shishinden, is believed to symbolise a palace. However, their effect is not only symbolic, they give depth to the expanse of courtyard.

The combination of Chinese and traditional Japanese architecture also marked the Heian domestic architecture with a pronounced simplicity. The nobility developed an ideal type of mansion to which the term Shinden-zukuri was applied. The shinden mansion and its garden occupied an area of about three and a half acres (one cho). The complex of buildings was arranged around a symmetrical pattern, at the centre of which was the main hall, shinden, which faced south on to the garden. There were three residential halls, tai-no-ya, to the north, east and west of the main hall, which were linked by covered verandahs. The buildings were constructed from unpainted wood; they rested a few feet above the ground on pillars, were single-storeyed and had shingled bark roofs. The entire rectangular complex was enclosed by a stone wall.

The garden contained Chinese features—the artificial hills and mountains, standing stones, a lake and islands reached by an ornamental bridge and two streams. White sand would have been spread over flat areas of the garden, for it shone like the sea in the moonlight. To the south of the lake would be the fishing hall, tsuridono, and the spring hall, izumidono (izumo meaning spring or fountainhead). The images of ocean and river were obviously favoured, judging by the extensive use of water, which was in abundant supply from the Kamo and Katsura rivers. Two parallel streams entered the shinden compound from the east, wound their way into the lake, and passed out in a south-westerly direction, often meandering under the buildings and corridors. Ornamental bridges could sometimes be found along the corridors connecting the pavilions.

The arrangement of the buildings allowed a closer relationship between house and garden, which was further linked by the streams; the garden and buildings became integral parts of each other. The Chinese palaces, on which the arrangement of the shinden buildings was based, faced across a courtyard to the entrance gate; the garden was confined to the back of the building. But the Japanese emphasised the importance of the garden by placing it at the front of the main hall; sometimes the hall was built on the very banks of the lake.

The structure of the building itself encouraged a closer, more intimate relationship with the garden. The house could be opened out so that there were no barriers between interior and exterior. The garden landscape could become an extension of the living area. The walls consisted of a series of shutters which could be opened and bamboo blinds which could be raised, so that the interior opened out directly on to the garden. Such an arrangement provided immediate contact with the changing seasons, which would be impressed on the mood of the people. As the mood reflected the season, the image of the garden reflected the image of the people, and as the physical barriers between exterior and interior were removed, so the sense of identity was strengthened.

Much of our knowledge of Heian Kyo is derived from The Tale of Genji, an epic love story by Murasaki Shikibu, and the Pillow Book of Sei Shonagon. Both Murasaki Shikibu and Sei Shonagon were ladies of the Heian court, in the early eleventh century. The Tale of Genji was illustrated in a famous set of ten scroll paintings (Genji-monogatari-e-maki) in the twelfth century. The link between house and garden was clearly demonstrated in these paintings,

In the illustration of the heroine's death scene in the Genji scrolls there is no visible demarcation between the room and the windswept garden with its desolate clover bushes; and the poems that she, Genji, and the other characters exchange are all built about images taken from the surrounding world of nature to which their emotions are so closely attuned.★

The Tale of Genji describes a society where status was acquired by virtue of aesthetic and artistic attainment, not through intellectual achievement. 'Never among people of exquisite cultivation and lively intelligence, have purely intellectual pursuits played so small a part,' wrote Arthur Waley. The cultivation of beauty was the predominant ambition. Letters and notes were written as poetry; poetic ability and standards of calligraphy

★ See I. Morris: *The World of the Shining Prince*, p. 49.

[33]

were admired and scrutinised. To play music and dance well were necessary requirements of the nobility. The performance of stylised dances was part of the duty of a government official. This exceptionally elegant society displayed a highly-developed sense of colour.

The Empress was wearing the usual scarlet robe, under which she had kimonos of light plum, light green and yellow rose. His Majesty's outer robe was made of grape-coloured brocade; underneath he had a willow green kimono and below that, one of pure white—all most unusual and up to date in both design and colour. ... Lady Nakazukasa's robe which was also of grape-coloured brocade, hung loosely over a plain jacket of green and cherry.★

The garden and the choice of plants were obvious means for the expression of such refined colour sensibility. From the descriptions of the gardens, the importance of the season and its particular atmosphere is also evident. Referring to Genji's mansion, Murasaki wrote:

He effected great improvement in the appearance of the grounds by a judicious handling of knoll and lake, for though such features were already there in abundance, he found it necessary here to cut away a slope, there to dam a stream, that each occupant of the various quarters might look out of her windows upon such a prospect as pleased her best. To the south-east he raised the level of the ground, and on this bank planted a profusion of early flowering trees. At the foot of this slope the lake curved with especial beauty, and in the foreground, just beneath the windows, he planted borders of cinquefoil, of red plum, cherry, wistaria, kerria, rock azalea and other such plants as are at their best in springtime, for he knew that Murasaki (his favourite) was especially a lover of the spring; while here and there in places where they would not obstruct his plan, autumn beds were cleverly interwoven with the rest.†

Appreciation of stones and rock was also apparent, and there were many well-shaped boulders to be found

in and around the capital. When describing two islands in a garden lake, Murasaki wrote:

They discovered to their delight that the shape of every little ledge and crag of stone had been as carefully devised as if a painter had traced there with his brush.★

The garden stream featured in the festivities of the court; for at the Winding Water banquets, guests would pick out cups of wine floating in the stream, recite a poem and then return the cup to the water. On the garden lakes, guests would be rowed in magnificent barges, carved and painted with the dragons and the heads of mythical birds. It was as if in front of the pure and simple lines of the main hall, the garden became an elaborate stage set, where myth and fantasy could erupt in dazzling colour against an idealised, dream landscape.

However fantastic the setting of the landscape garden might be, the inspiration was to be found in the native scenery. Even though the style of the garden was derived from the Chinese models, the images projected in the garden were firmly rooted in the mountains, coastline and islands of Japan itself. At Kawara-in, the river-bank villa of Minamoto no Toru, the Minister of the Left, a garden was constructed in A.D. 857 to suggest the bay of Matsushima in Mutsu province. The bay, one of Japan's Three Scenic Wonders, is a small archipelago of craggy, pine-covered islands.

Matsushima was believed to be the first place in Japan where salt was extracted by boiling sea water; the nearby town is Shiogama, meaning salt cauldron. To complete his fantasy, Minamoto no Toru ordered sea water to be brought from the coast, thirty miles away, and while gallons were boiled in a salt kiln, he and his guests could admire the smoke wafting across the sky, enjoy the scent of the burning wood, and imagine themselves to be by the rugged coast to the far north. Sumiyoshi beach, in Settsu province, was suggested in a pebbled shore in the garden of Taira no Shigechika in the south of the city. At Rokujo-in, Onakaomi no Sukechika, a contemporary of Murasaki, had a long

★ From the Diary of Murasaki Shikibu, *Murasaki Shikibu Nikki*, edited by Mochizuki Sekkyo, Tokyo, 1929, pp. 113–14. See I. Morris: *The World of the Shining Prince*, p. 206.

† From *The Tale of Genji*, Part III, A Wreath of Cloud, Ch. 3, pp. 430–1 in A. Waley translation. Also quoted in Loraine Kuck: *The World of the Japanese Garden*, p. 87.

★ *The Tale of Genji*, Part III, Ch. 6, pp. 478–9 in A. Waley translation. Also in Loraine Kuck: *The World of the Japanese Garden*, p. 88.

Kara-e, the continental style which was used for illustration of Chinese legends and landscapes, though practised until the twelfth century, was confined to official and religious painting. Kose-no-Kanoaka is frequently mentioned in the records of the time as the first master of Japanese painting, and as such was especially respected. He is considered one of the originators of Yamato-e. As well as being a great painter, he was Superintendent of the Imperial Garden, the Shinsen-en, the Sacred Spring Garden, and was responsible for arranging some of the rocks; he also worked on the gardens of Kan-in and Saga-in.

In contrast to the austerity of the Kokyo, the Shinsen-en was a huge, informal lake garden. It was laid out in A.D. 800, shortly after the founding of the capital, and is considered to have been one of the earliest of the shinden-style gardens. Occupying about twenty-five acres (8 cho), the garden was dominated by an enormous lake with a shoreline of white sand. In the centre of the lake, accessible by an ornamental bridge, was an island. There was a hill covered in maples, willows and cherry trees. Water had been used in the garden on an ambitious, unprecedented scale. Its source was the Divine Spring, which was situated in a corner of the garden. By the mouth of the spring was a waterfall. Deer roamed the grounds and doves and waterfowl were in abundance. The landscape was as natural as the soft beauty of the hills around the city. It was constructed much like the image of the landscape painting, and must have inspired Kose-no-Kanoaka, who is known to have painted it.

Another great lake garden of the period was that of the Emperor Saga, which was built on the northern outskirts of the city. It was built in the early ninth century as a retreat, following the Emperor's retirement. A lake covering almost six acres was constructed by damming a stream. The lake once contained a line of five islands; this was a characteristic of Heian gardens. The islands were known as night mooring stones, yo-domari, which suggested a line of ships anchored in a harbour. There is also a waterfall at one end of the lake, which some believe was always dry. Possibly it was designed as a dry cascade, kare taki, which suggests that water will resume flowing with the next rain. The element

peninsula built in the garden lake, which was planted with pine trees, after the windswept, twisted trees at Amanohashidate on the Inland Sea.

The focus had changed; the Japanese no longer turned to the continent for inspiration. It was the pattern to be repeated in later history; after a period of great foreign influence, the national consciousness emerged again.★ The gates to the mainland were closing. By A.D. 894 the final diplomatic mission to China was withdrawn. The great T'ang dynasty was in decline. A new phase in Japanese history had begun. Like the gardens of Heian Kyo, secular painting from the middle of the ninth century was inspired by the native landscape. The towering rock pinnacles of the T'ang landscapes were replaced by the softer, rounder hills of the surrounding area of the capital.

A style of painting known as Yamato-e (painting in the Japanese manner) became increasingly popular.

★ See I. Morris: *The World of the Shining Prince*, p. 24. Also by the same author: *Nationalism and the Right Wing in Japan*, p. 123.

[37]

of water was established by suggestion, not by its actual presence. The strength of the image is a result of what the designers omitted, not what was added. Adjacent to the nearby waterfall house was a rock arrangement designed by another painter, Kudara no Kawanari.

One of the major sources of information on the Heian gardens is the Sakuteiki, the Treatise on Garden Making. It was written by Tachibana Toshitsuna (1027–1094), a son of Fujiwara Yorimichi, a leading statesman. The first chapter of the book deals with the construction of gardens in the shinden style; details on ponds, streams, islands, waterfalls and plants are given. However, the book is highly dogmatic and threatens terrible misfortunes on those who break the established rules. It mentions Kose-no-Hirotaka, the grandson of the originator of Yamato-e painting, himself a leading painter of his day, in charge of the Painting Office at the court, as being well-informed on garden taboos. By the eleventh century many of the garden principles were clouded with superstition.

When the capital was founded, the city was planned according to geomantic beliefs; the art of Feng Shui was evidently well-known to the Japanese. When communication with the mainland was broken, and the Japanese turned in on themselves, sealing their independence as an island race, the meaning of such beliefs was lost and their power as images was misunderstood. Only the empty vestiges of the geomantic tradition remained and were misapplied in alien contexts.

For example, the concept of Four Quarters, Shijin-so, which had been applied by the Chinese to the location of the cities, houses, tombs and the plan of gardens, attributed the symbols of the White Tiger to the east, the Azure Dragon to the west, the Black Tortoise to the north and the Red Phoenix to the south. The most auspicious site would have a stream on the east, a path on the west, a hill to the north and a pond to the south. The symbolic creatures would be satisfied by such positioning, and good fortune would ensue from the balance thus obtained. This concept was then reinterpreted by the Heian gardeners, without foundation, as the planting of nine willow trees on the east, seven maples on the west, three cypress to the north and nine Judas trees to the south. The constraint of such ideas, when interpreted as rules, indicated the growth of rigid dogma. When such concepts had to be dictated and listed as they were in the Sakuteiki, the images were no longer part of a vital tradition—they were dead.

Living within such a confined world as Heian Kyo must have been oppressive at times. The desire to escape and explore the country at large, was channelled into the fantasy of the garden. It is unlikely that Minamoto no Toru, with his salt kiln in his garden, would ever have made the long, hard journey up to Matsushima itself. It was much safer to stay at home and cultivate the delicate comforts of the resplendent court. The court ritual established an order in the daily life of the capital; it provided a framework for an elaborate existence, sometimes so unreal in its isolation that it appears almost theatrical. Cut off from the original source of inspiration, the beauty of the landscape, the wild and remote scenery of Japan itself, out of touch with the rough reality of the feudal peasantry—the atmosphere was unhealthy. Behind the opulent façade of the court were quarrels and intrigue. Decadence was rendering the court ineffective as a power. The dream was about to burst.

Out in the provinces, life was unsettled. Away from the sheltered world of the capital, the warrior governed by the sword. In the city, the aristocratic families juggled for power and the supremacy of the Emperor was overshadowed by that of the great Fujiwara family. The established order was challenged and the central administration was breaking down. The provincial lords were gathering together to defend their estates from marauding hordes; rival clans engaged in bitter feuds. In the tenth and eleventh centuries, Japan was the scene of brutal uprisings and vicious warfare. The foundations of power were changing; a great storm was about to break.

Against such a background a new dream was taking shape. It was a dream of a better world and of rebirth in paradise, which was realised through the cult of Amida Buddha. A system of salvation and rebirth in the Pure Land of the West, Saiho Jodo, the paradise of Amida, was spread by the monk Eshin-sozu through his book *Birth in the Land of Purity*, Ojo-yoshu, which was based on the Kan-Maryoju-kyo sutra and was published in A.D. 985. When destruction was rife and life brief, the promise of a better world held great appeal. As the social order crumbled, the dream of the Pure Land in the West offered consolation, reassurance and hope. When the stability of the court itself was threatened, the aristocracy too found comfort in the possibility of a future paradise, where the elegance of their life style might be continued.

The image of this paradise could be contained in the mandala (Jap. mandara; Sanskrit mandala). The mandala was an archetypal symbol of the cosmos, in the form of a circle; it was a universal symbol of unity. Great significance was attributed to the mandala in Eastern religious painting, especially in the painting of the Tantric cults and of Tibetan Lamaism, where it was used as a figure on which to meditate. The conventional Japanese mandala was a painting of the Buddhist pantheon, at the centre of which was the principal Buddhist deity, Danichi-nyorai (Sanskrit Maha Vairocana). The sun-like Tantric deity Danichi-nyorai (Vairocana) represented the Shinto Sun Goddess, Amaterasu, who had been absorbed along with other Shinto deities into the Buddhist pantheon. The Buddhist deities of the mandala were arranged in concentric circles, taizo-kai (Sanskrit, Gharba dhatu), or a rectangle, kongo-kai (Sanskrit, Vajra dhatu), around the principal deity.

The symbol of the circle is most common in Buddhist art. As a symbol it can be interpreted as all-embracing, without beginning or end, yet it contains nothing; it frames the Void. However, the symbolic, cosmic circle is certainly not confined to the East, for many Western counterparts to the mandala exist. It is found in the rose windows of the cathedrals, in paintings of the Virgin surrounded by the four evangelists, in Dante's vision of the Saintly Throng in the form of the rose, and in the plan of the Holy City in the vision of St John the Divine. It can be traced in the ground-plans of temples of various religious origins, and even in the ground-plans of cities such as Rome★ or the walled cities of medieval Europe. The city itself became a projection of sacred balance or order as a result of such a plan. The sacred proportions of the architecture or the plans then elevated the inhabitants to a higher spiritual existence. It was with these exact intentions, that the Japanese then applied the mandala of paradise to the garden.

The gardens of the early Heian aristocracy reflected the structure of their social hierarchy, with the Emperor firmly seated at the top. The mountains of the gardens were compared to the Emperor, the rocks to his officials and the surrounding water to his courtiers. It was said that as the Emperor should be protected by his officials and close advisers from the intrigues of his courtiers, so the garden hills should be protected by the stones from the power of the water. The emphasis of the garden now changed; it represented not the Imperial court, but the sanctuary of Amida's paradise.

At the beginning of the eleventh century, the regent, Fujiwara Michinaga, an ardent devotee of Amida, built the temple of Hojoji. The temple itself was dedicated to Danichi-nyorai, whose image occupied the main hall. Amida was housed in the western hall and on the east, not the eastern Buddha, Yakushi, but the Five Wrathful Gods, Godaison, were housed. (According to the Tantric system these gods balanced the gods of mercy and love, such as Amida, by their ability to instil terror into the power of evil.)

★ See Plutarch's account of the founding of Rome.

Although Amida's position was secondary to that of Danichi-nyorai, Amida exercised greater power, and it was his hall that was the first to be dedicated. This arrangement aptly reflected the position at the court, where the title of the Emperor was only nominal, and real power lay with the man at his side, the Fujiwara regent. One of the court romances of the time, Eiga Monogatari, described the Hojoji as containing, 'columns with bases of ivory, roof ridges of red gold, gilded doors, platforms of crystal'. The trees were said to have leaves of pearl, gold and amber or lapis and there was a pool of gold and jade. In true Heian style, the dream was elaborate.

Conventionally the mandala of paradise contained seven features: sanzon-e, where the image of Amida was kept; horon-kyuden-e, the treasure hall; hochi-e, the treasure pond; juge-e, a holy place under the trees; bugaku-e, a place for dance and music; raibutsu-e, a place for saints; and koku-e, a place for angels and holy animals.

These features were ideally arranged either in a circle or a geometrical pattern, and formed the component parts of a mandala in much the same manner as a painting. However, the garden mandala allowed a certain freedom of expression, which could not be achieved within the two dimensions of the painting. There was greater space for more flexible design. Although the ideal form was the circle, it was still more important that the design merged with the topography or features of the landscape, than followed a perfect geometrical shape. The image was not mathematical but natural.

The complex of temple and garden that constituted the mandala could only be seen as a complete expression of paradise when viewed from above. Such a view was hypothetical; to experience the mandala in a moment in its entirety, as one could with a painting, it was necessary to project oneself to a point in space directly overhead. To see the picture as a whole one had to fly, and with dreams of paradise one was no longer tied to the earth.

Do I, then, belong to the heavens?
Why, if not so, should the heavens
Fix me thus with their ceaseless blue stare,
Luring me on, and my mind, higher
Ever higher, up into the sky,
Drawing me ceaselessly up
To heights far, far above the human?
Why, when balance has been strictly studied
And flight calculated with the best of reason
Till no aberrant element should, by rights, remain—
Why, still, should the lust for ascension
Seem, in itself, so close to madness?
Nothing is that can satisfy me;
Earthly novelty is too soon dulled;
I am drawn higher and higher, more unstable,
Closer and closer to the sun's effulgence.
Why do they burn me, these rays of reason,
Why do these rays of reason destroy me?
Villages below and meandering streams
Grow tolerable as our distance grows.

From Icarus, by Yukio Mishima★

The most celebrated monument to Amida is the Phoenix Hall of the Bjodoin temple, which was built just outside the capital at Uji, and has miraculously survived. It was the residence of Michinaga's son Fujiwara no Yorimichi (992–1074) who, as was the custom, kept a hall dedicated to Amida at his home. The entire structure of the buildings has been designed to represent a phoenix about to take flight; the main hall being the body of the phoenix, the adjacent two-storeyed halls at the sides, the wings, and the extension at the back of the building being the tail.

You face the hall across a pond, once covered in lotus blossom. The sweeping curve of the roof, on the ridge of which stand two gilded bronze phoenix, has the lightness and power of the bird in flight, its wings reflected in the water. No better symbol of hope could have been chosen than the flight of the phoenix; a dream of soaring beauty rising from the fire. Between the vermilion pillars of the main hall, staring out across the water, sits a superb gilded wooden statue of the Amida Buddha, the work of Jocho—a sculptor of genius. The serene calm of the Buddha's expression is backed by a writhing halo of clouds and flames; the extreme tran-

★ Icarus by Yukio Mishima, published in *Sun and Steel*, translated by John Bester, published by Harper and Row, and Kodansha International 1970.

[40]

quillity and its opposite, the violent fire, are in perfect balance.

On the walls and panels of the doors within the main hall are nine paintings representing the nine versions of the descent of Amida (raigo). These paintings have not been executed with the formality of the conventional mandala. Instead, Amida is seen with his accompanying procession of Bodhisattvas, who are playing drums and lutes, hovering against a background of paradise, which is unmistakably inspired by the soft, green hills around the capital. The landscape on each of the four walls represents one of the four seasons, complete with details such as thatched cottages, horses grazing or drinking from a winding river, a boatload of firewood, cherry blossom and pine trees against the spreading, green space of pine-covered hills.

Behind the glorious façade of the temple in paradise, the image within, which decorates the hall of Amida, is simple and natural; it is drawn directly from the landscape of the vicinity. Though the imagination had reached high up into the clouds, an image of paradise could be found in the immediate, familiar surroundings. The steps, leading down from the front of the Phoenix Hall to a small area of gravel, are flanked by two shrubs and before the steps, in front of the water, there now stands a single stone lantern. The garden itself is reduced in scale from the extensive landscapes of the shinden mansions; no path follows the edge of the pool, and no stream winds into it. The pool no longer represents a far-off seashore; it is lined with willow, lotus and iris; plants to be found locally, not along the coast. The celestial garden, though fantastic in concept, is direct and simple in execution. Even more than before, the power of the garden lay not in what it actually represented, but in what it suggested.

The imagination, instead of rising from the fire like the phoenix, had flown too high, and like Icarus it had to fall. On the wings of the phoenix the imagination had indeed soared, but not even the sanctuary of Amida's paradise offered protection from the fire that had only just been lit.

The provincial warrior leaders were originally introduced into the power struggles of the court, as weapons with which to settle the internal disputes. The force they represented was powerful enough to upset the precarious *status quo* of the capital. Two provincial families, the Taira and the Minamoto, then emerged as the figureheads of the warrior classes. The effective rule of the nation lay in their hands and bitter rivalry was inevitable. After two wars, in 1156 and 1159–1160, the victorious Taira clan established their leader, Taira Kiyomori, in Kyoto. He then ousted the Fujiwara and himself held the key position of power at the side of the Emperor.

By remaining in the capital, the Taira were then vulnerable to exactly the same factors that had eroded the power of the Fujiwara; they were cutting themselves off from the backbone of their strength, the provincial lords, and succumbing to the allure of overindulgence in seclusion at the court. In 1180 the Minamoto rose to challenge the supremacy of the Taira, and for five years a bitter civil war between the two clans ensued. It resulted in the deaths of the Taira leaders and of the boy Emperor, a grandson of Kiyomori. The head of the Minamoto, Yoritomo, then occupied the position of control. Having learned from the example of the Taira, Yoritomo wasted no time in the capital. He left the Imperial court together with the Fujiwara to struggle to preserve their prestige in the capital, and moved to establish a military centre of power at Kamakura.

After the fire and destruction of civil war, a new virility was injected into the culture. A certain respect for simplicity accompanied the fierce warrior spirit, in stark contrast to the lavish decadence of the court. The time was ripe for fresh influences; the Minamoto government encouraged relations with the continent and the seal of isolation was broken. As a sign of the revived link with the mainland, the great monasteries of Nara, which had been sacked by the Taira army in 1180, were reconstructed. Chinese records of the twelfth century mention the arrival of Japanese ships on several occasions.

Besides the painting of the Sung dynasty, for the first time the Japanese came into contact with Zen Buddhism (Sanskrit Dhyana; Chinese Ch'an), which was introduced to Japan by the monk Min-an Eisai (1141–

1187), after two journeys to China in 1168 and 1187. The developing Japanese imagination was to be channelled to a profound depth, by the vigour of the military tradition of Kamakura, the stimulating beauty of Sung art and the discipline of Zen.

Kamakura, a perfect military site, mountains on three sides, sea on the fourth, was also the site for five great Zen Buddhist temples. The warriors of Kamakura were strongly attracted to Zen and generously patronised the temples, for Buddhism and the samurai code of Bushido had a common symbol—the sword.

The sword has thus a double office to perform; to destroy anything that opposes the will of its owner and to sacrifice all impulses that arise from the instinct of self-preservation. The one relates itself to the spirit of patriotism or sometimes to militarism, while the other has a religious connotation of loyalty and self-sacrifice.★

The art of swordsmanship is practised with the discipline of Zen (see Takano Shigeyoshi, Ch. 2) and the manufacture of the sword is an art, which has strong spiritual associations, for it involves ritual invocation of the Shinto gods and consecration of the workshop. The art was at its peak during the Kamakura period. One legend records how a sword of the master swordsmith of Kamakura, Masamune, and one made by his disciple, Muramasa, were compared by being placed in a stream. Every leaf that flowed against the disciple's blade was split, but the leaves avoided the blade of the master; his blade had a strength sharper than steel—a strength derived from Zen. Power and solidity were imparted to the highly-developed sensibility of the Japanese, as Zen permeated an attitude to life, which was to find expression in art of sublime beauty.

So there developed at Kamakura a curious combination of the martial arts and the teaching of the elusive, indefinable attitude of Zen. With great industry, the temples of this Buddhist sect were being erected alongside the vermilion walls of a Shinto shrine dedicated to Hachiman, the god of war. True to principles of adaptation these temples merged into the landscape of the surrounding hills, neither clashing with the landscape nor being dominated by it. The eye passes over the bare,

★ See D. T. Suzuki: *Zen and Japanese Culture*, p. 89.

unvarnished wooden pillars supporting the heavy temple roofs, which appear by means of their gentle curves to be floating weightless, suspended against the background of the forest, reaching up towards the sky.

The followers of the cult of Amida had literally inhabited their visions of paradise—if one was to obtain salvation, one had to live within the mandala itself; so the Hojoji and the Byodo-in were in fact Fujiwara residences, not separate places of worship. Under the influence of Zen, the architecture of the temple moved still closer to the style of domestic buildings. Since Zen emphasised the omnipresence of Buddha,

The sound of the wind in the pine trees or the roar of the waterfall—these were voices chanting the sutras; the shape of a mountain, of a tree, of a stone—these were images of Buddha. Why should man compete with them? Four walls and a roof could make a temple, and an abstract garden could express all the truths of Zen.★

Just as painting was practised by the Zen monks as a spiritual exercise, it was they who became the great exponents of the art of gardening, which though inspired by religious concepts, had previously been restricted to the villas of the nobility; they now applied the art to the grounds of the temples. They were to instil the gardens not with the conventions of the Buddhist

★ Teiji Itoh: *The Roots of Japanese Architecture*.

[43]

pantheon in a formal mandala, but with the exuberant vitality of natural form.

Yoritomo, on a campaign in the far north, was deeply impressed by the last of the formal Heian temples, Moetsuji, which had been built by the Fujiwara at Hirai-zumi. On the same axis as the gate of Moetsuji was a bridge which reached an island in a small lake; another bridge joined the island to the shore opposite the main hall. At the sites of the two terminal pavilions, large garden stones still remain. A stream passed from behind the buildings, branched under the corridors and entered the pond through the stones on either side. On his return to Kamakura, Yoritomo started the construction of a magnificent garden, modelled on Moetsuji at the temple of Eifuku-ji, which was well documented in the chronicle of the time, the Mirror of the East.

Under the direction of the priest, Jogen, stones were piled around the edge of the site and a lake was exca-vated. It is recorded that cherry and apricot trees were used, but their planting was too unimportant, compared with the positioning of the stones, to warrant any de-scription. Of great significance was the emphasis placed on the stonework. It was evident that the laying down of the stones was like the establishment of a skeleton for the body of the garden. Though nothing remains today, ex-cept a site overgrown with weeds, in its time the garden was described as being 'as beautiful as Amida's paradise'.

At the same time as Zen was introduced, the cult of Amida was by no means replaced by the new sect. The memory of a savage civil war must have been strongly imprinted, and the hope for salvation through the divine intervention of Amida was reinforced by the preaching of the monk, Honen (1132–1212), who founded the Jodo (Pure Land) sect. Though the plastic representation of Amida was of less importance to Honen with his reformed Amidism, in 1252 the greatest

[44]

effigy of Amida, the colossal bronze Buddha of Kamakura Daibatsu was erected by public subscription, and remains to this day as testimony to the powerful appeal of the merciful god. It faces out to sea, calm and passive, appearing as if undaunted by the tidal waves that have swamped it. The cult of Amida evidently continued to flourish and still today followers of the sect practise 'nenbutsu', which is the repetition for long periods of time of the phrase 'Namu Amida Butsu', meaning 'homage to Amida Buddha', in the hope of rebirth in paradise.

The Pure Land of Amida and the more abstruse experience of Zen are both expressed side by side at the garden of Saihoji temple in Kyoto. It extends over the side of a mountain, at the bottom of which is a lake, the golden pond (ogonchi). The lake garden is based on a style inspired by the paradise of the Jodo sect, and is similar to the style of the earlier Heian shinden gardens.

The lake contains scattered rocks and an island; its winding shore is lined with soft, moss-covered banks. However, the design shows no trace of the formal conventions of the mandala. The garden now appears like a dark, damp wood. Time has weathered the landscape, so that any hint of calculated design has been submerged beneath the abundant growth of moss that carpets the ground, and the lichens that lie in patches on the stones and cover the trunks of trees.

During the Meiji period (1868–1911) the finances of the temple were too low to afford the upkeep of the garden and its subsequent neglect, together with its sheltered position and rich clay soil, encouraged a profusion of different mosses to spread; over forty different varieties are said to have been established. This very neglect effected such richness and diversity of colour and texture, that the garden acquired a mood that no gardener could have cultivated, yet to maintain the mood the gardener employs his utmost skill. The garden is now also known as Kokedera, the garden of mosses.

Climbing the slope above the lake you pass under a gateway, the Kokojan, and rough stone steps lead you up into yet another garden; a garden of subtle suggestion, with no trace of imitative representation. To one side of the path, embedded in the moss, is the first group of stones. Rounded stones with rough surfaces lie next to smooth, flat-topped stones in balanced arrangement, which to the casual observer might appear random. The soft, undulating moss laps the stones like water. Some authorities claim that the stones represent Mount Sumeru, others that they form the image of the tortoise. The trap of symbolic interpretation is therefore apparent. If you view the stones as a tortoise basking in a pool, or as the holy mountain rising from the ocean, either interpretation is valid. The image was not intended to be forced, it was designed to be suggestive. It is the experience that Zen emphasised, not the concept of the experience. (Your own experience is what matters, not what you are told to see.)

A shallow pool is lodged in the hillside, bordered by rocks, through which the water trickles. Higher still, enormous, rugged boulders follow the slope, many of them flat-topped like giant steps; they fall to a 'pool' of moss, enclosed by smaller rocks. This dry cascade has

the power of the rushing stream and the force of the waterfall, yet no torrents of water race down the hill. The great blocks of granite have been left as if emerging from the erosion of the constant flow of pounding water. Out of the silence of the dark, overshadowing trees, the cascade can turn your ears to a roaring echo. Out of the static forms of the rocks, dappled with lichen, appearing immovable, a sense of swirling motion is achieved. This arrangement epitomises the boldness, vigour and strength that the artist now applied to the landscape.

The garden is attributed to the Zen priest, Muso Soseki (also known as Muso Kokushi) (1275–1351). He is said to have built the garden in 1339 for Fujiwara no Chikahide. It was a product of a turbulent age. The Kamakura shogunate,* weakened by Mongol invasions

* The shogun was the title of the effective ruler of Japan, the head of government, who did not actually replace the Emperor, but assumed power. The shogunate was established by Minamoto Yoritomo in 1192 during the Kamakura period and lasted until the Meiji Restoration of 1868 returned direct power to the Emperor.

from Korea, had been overthrown in 1333, in an attempt to restore the direct government of the Emperor. The movement was known as the Kemmu Restoration, and was backed by the leading general of the time, Ashikaga Takauji. In 1336 the general himself assumed power in Kyoto and appointed a new Emperor of his own choosing. The country was again plunged into disorder and civil war between the rival Northern and Southern courts erupted; it was to last fifty years. Fujiwara no Chikahide was a powerful member of the Ashikaga government, and Muso, who was held in great esteem at the time, also served as a government adviser. Beneath the calm of the garden exterior there runs a forceful current which perhaps reflects something of the stormy period in which Muso lived. It also hints at the power of the natural forces that lurk under the quiet surface.

Saihoji demonstrates several important developments in garden style. The use of stones, which was documented earlier in the Mirror of the East with reference to Eifuku-ji, was now being employed with great skill. The stones had been brought from a distance, as no rocks are to be found on the hillside except in the garden; they had also been selected with particular care. Unlike previous gardens, the tall upright stone so familiar as a mountain image is not used. The focus of the vision was becoming more concentrated.

In contrast to the more conventional Pure Land of Amida in the lower garden, which represented a clearly-defined paradise in its entirety—a complete landscape— the upper garden is orientated around details—the steps, the pool, the cascade. Like a cameraman with a zoom lens, the eye was being drawn closer into the image; the previous paradise vision was seen from the clouds, the new Zen-inspired vision had its foundations firmly on the ground. There was no need for a great garden lake, when the power of water could be seen in the small pool or the cascade. By following the process of reduction and moving closer to the abstract, the artist was getting nearer to the raw image. When the pool was made of moss and the cascade of dry stone, the process of reduction was nearly complete.

Some authorities believe that the garden of Saihoji dates from a period before Muso's time, and that he

[48]

only effected certain changes on an already existing structure. Nevertheless, Muso is considered an inspired architect of change and is deeply respected as one of the great gardener-priests. He is also said to be responsible for the gardens of Nanzenji and Tenryuji in Kyoto. Though his role as the original designer of the latter garden is likewise disputed, it is recorded that in 1342 Muso was instructed by Ashikaga Takauji to convert a former imperial shinden estate to a Zen temple, now known as Tenryuji. The conversion marks the transition from the more formal, symmetrically-arranged shinden style to the irregular but more compact shoin style that was emerging at the time.

The abbot's residence at Tenryuji faces south-west to a small pond, with no island, on the far banks of which is a dry cascade. Below the cascade is a narrow bridge, resting on two jagged slabs of stone. To cross the bridge one would walk slowly and carefully; its narrowness and irregularity encouraged one to linger. The scale of the pond had been reduced; its purpose was neither representational nor purely decorative. The garden was moving further from the original extensive paradise through which one strolled. It was designed to be experienced as a complete composition from a point of rest in the abbot's residence. The design encouraged contemplation. The influence of Zen was becoming strikingly apparent.

The restrained beauty of Saihoji was the inspiration for one of the last great paradise gardens. Ashikaga Yoshimitsu (1358–1408), who brought an end to the civil war between the rival courts, temporarily restored order and firmly established the Ashikaga shogunate,★ was a great patron of the arts and a Sinophile. He surrounded himself with Sung treasures and promoted relations with the new Ming dynasty (1368–1644) of China. He was deeply impressed by Saihoji, which moved him to create his own retreat, Rokuonji, the Deer Park in the north of Kyoto; it was so named after the deer park at Sarnath, outside Benares, on the river Ganges, the site of Guatama Buddha's first sermon. The retreat is now more commonly known as Kinkakuji, the Temple of the Golden Pavilion.

For a site, Yoshimitsu chose that of an earlier, splendid temple, built by the thirteenth-century leader, Saionji Kintsune, which had suffered from neglect and fallen into decay. Beside the already existing lake, Kokyo, the Mirror Lake, in 1397 he built a magnificent, three-storeyed pavilion, amalgamating a number of different architectural styles. Its overall appearance by the water's edge is similar to the Chinese pavilions, as illustrated in Sung paintings, but the shingle roof and the original unpainted wood of the framework of the building follows the unmistakable native tradition. The top floor, a Zen chapel, has bell-shaped windows with cusped arches, typical of the Zen temple. The different styles have been integrated to demonstrate remarkable flowing proportions of architectural harmony. The ceiling of the uppermost storey was gilded, after which the building acquired the title of the 'golden pavilion'. The original structure was destroyed by fire in 1950. The reconstructed replica is faithful in every way, except the outside of the two upper storeys has been covered in gold leaf. Though dazzling, especially in the snow when the gold blazes against the white background, the present building is not true to the simplicity of the original, unimposing, Zen-influenced conception.

The estate covers an area of four and a half acres, a third of which is the lake. A peninsula and long island divide the lake. The inner half, that nearest to the pavilion, is filled with five small islands and a number of rocks, some of which are enormous—seventeen oxen were required to move one of them. The outer half of the lake is almost empty except for a few very small islands. The design creates a sense of space; it forms its own distant horizon. The skilful suggestion of the ocean had developed considerably from the original lakes of the old shinden gardens. Trees line the shores of the lake, not restricting or dwarfing it, but fitting perfectly into the scale of the garden. A path winds around the edge of the lake, yet many of the details of the garden, such as the rock arrangements of the islands, are seen best from a boat.

Two springs nestle among large rocks in the side of the hill behind the pavilion. At the top of the hill, hidden

★ The period of the Ashikaga shogunate (1399–1573) is also referred to as the Muromachi period, after the Muromachi district of Kyoto where Ashikaga Takauji first established his government.

in the trees, is a secluded tea house, Kan'un-tei, copied from the Shuken-tei tea house high up by the dry pool and cascade of Saihoji. Over the centuries silt has filled areas of the lake, which now lie wooded and covered with moss. What were once rocky islands in the water, now stand as dry boulders between the trees. Yoshimitsu is believed to have designed the garden himself; with great skill he created a world of spaciousness and grandeur, balanced by delicacy and restraint. The pavilion and garden stand as a magnificent gesture of paradise, to counter the misery that plagues the history of medieval Japan.

Beside the garden path there is a waterfall, the Dragon Gate cascade. The water pours down on to a 'Carp' stone, from which it showers like a fountain. Though the waterfall dates from the earlier garden of Kintsune, the symbol of the carp is appropriate to Yoshimitsu. The carp, because it is a fish that can swim against the current, is a symbol traditionally endowed with strength and perseverance. Despite the climate of instability and violence that characterises the period, through the garden Yoshimitsu expressed a calm sensitivity, attuned to a flow that was constant and ran deeper than the currents of politics.

The predominant influence of Saihoji was superimposed on the framework of the Pure Land garden by Yoshimitsu's grandson, the shogun Yoshimasa (1435–1490). Like his grandfather, Yoshimasa never failed to be stirred by the powerful beauty of the moss garden, which he visited regularly. In 1482 he built his retreat, Higashiyamadono, among the eastern hills of the capital. When he died, the garden became a temple in his memory, which was called Jisho-ji, after his spiritual title of Jisho. The garden is commonly known as Ginkakuji, in reference to the Silver Pavilion which he built. He was drawn closer than his grandfather to the implications of Zen, and not having the means to indulge in the same luxury, he left a more modest and simple retreat.

A lake garden at the foot of the hills reaches up to a higher garden on the slopes above, which was discovered after excavations in 1931. The lake, the Brocade Mirror, Kinkyo-cho, forms the treasure pond, hochi-e, of the conventional paradise garden. Azalea bushes and trees are reflected in the water of the pond, which is comparatively small. The cultivated trees of the garden rise up to meet the wild forest of the hillside. Access to a small island in the lake is obtained by two bridges, one of which consists of two rough slabs of stone, like the bridge of Tenryuji; the other, which was originally an arched wooden bridge, the Dragon Back bridge, has been replaced by a huge, single piece of granite. Flat-topped rocks lie around the base of the island, reminiscent of those at Saihoji. A stream runs down the hillside into the lake, broken along its course by a cascade called the Moon Washing Spring, Sengetsugen, as if the moon itself was bathed in the water of the pool beneath it.

There were originally twelve buildings in the garden, of which only two remain. The Togudo, the East Seeking Hall, is a temple for Amida, at the back of which is a small tea room. Yoshimasa delighted in this small, square chamber of four and a half tatami★ where the tea ceremony, cha-no-yu, was held under the guidance of the tea master Shuko. This arrangement reflects both the strong spiritual associations of the tea cult and the remarkable degree to which the temple had been secularised. It would have been unheard of, before the Ashikaga period, to have combined the temple with a chamber for secular functions in the same building, as in the Togudo and also the Golden Pavilion, where the first floor was a recreational hall for poetry parties and receptions, and the upper floor a Zen chapel. In the water in front of the Togudo grow lotuses, the flowers of paradise.

The other surviving building is the Silver Pavilion itself. It is a two-storeyed structure, modelled on the Ruriden, a pavilion that once stood at Saihoji. The lower floor, the Soul Emptying Hall, Shinko-den, was used for zazen (meditation). The upper floor with bell-

★ tatami: The tatami is a thick straw mat of a standardised size, approximately six feet by three feet. It has a woven straw covering and a straw filling. It was introduced in the late fifteenth century with the shoin style of architecture. Until then the straw mat had been used as a cushion on the wooden floors. It became a standard unit of area, which determined the proportions of the room, and is still used as such today. Four and a half tatami was a common size for a tea room, the half tatami accounting for the area of the sunken charcoal brazier in the centre of the room.

GINKAKUJI.

shaped windows contains an image of Kannon, the Buddhist goddess of mercy. From the balcony on the upper floor, Yoshimasa is said to have watched the moon rise over the hills. He would then have seen the silver light cast over the garden that spread beneath him. From that point of rest, he would see the islands silhouetted against the ripples of the water and the dark shadows of the hills behind like towering mountains, full of dark mystery, rising over an ocean.

Kinkakuji and Ginkakuji stand like sun and moon. The Silver Pavilion, smaller and simpler than its golden counterpart, is surrounded by lunar images. It is extra-ordinary to imagine a garden recorded through history in terms of its beauty by night. In the early seventeenth century much of the estate of Ginkakuji was reconstructed, and from that period date two of the features that are most conspicuous in the garden today. In front of the Silver Pavilion, beside the lake, stands a cone of white sand about six feet high, its top flattened, so that the cone shape is not quite completed. Its image needs no explanation—it is not just the image of a mountain, it is clearly the volcano. It is called Kogetsudai, the Moon Facing Height.

Next to the cone is a raised plateau of white sand

[52]

about two feet high. Its perimeter is irregularly shaped and it spreads to the front of the main hall (hondo) of the temple compound. The surface of the sand is raked in strips so that areas of smooth, unraked sand alternate with strips of furrowed sand. The wave-like image is clear; its title is Ginshandan, the Sea of Silver Sand. Though the sand features were not created by Yoshimasa, references to a sea of silver sand were made before the garden was reconstructed and it is probable that an area of sand existed in the original design. An important step was about to be taken, which is revealed in these unusual features—the image was moving towards the abstract.

About fifteen years before Yoshimasa finally built his retreat, he had made initial preparations for the project, but in 1467 fighting broke out in the very heart of the capital, the fashionable Muromachi district, and he had to abandon his plans. When he eventually returned to the proposed retreat, Japan had suffered ten years of the most destructive civil war that had yet been experienced—the Onin War (1467–1477). Except for the Byodo-in, which was outside the city, very few of the great temples and residences remained unscathed from the devastation of the period. Drought and famine racked

the oppressed and overtaxed peasant population. Against the backcloth of flames and human misery, the Pure Land continued to offer the path to salvation, but its paradise was tinged with the spirit of Zen, which was growing still stronger.

Ironically, at the time of greatest social upheaval and distress, Japanese art was about to rise to heights of unprecedented beauty. It was the very violence that moved the artist to such purity, calm and detachment. At the same time the Zen way to spiritual enlightenment was stripped of all orthodox religious connotations. Spiritual experience was found in secular aesthetics and in the patterns of the landscape, the forest, the mountain and the sea. The gardener's vision was sharpened and could express such patterns in rock, moss and sand. His image had been reduced; the identity was approaching completion. His expression turned now to the pure abstraction of landscape.

[55]

From Sand to the Sea

The Zen master Lin Chi (Jap. Rinzai, d. 867) gave this advice, 'When it is time to get dressed, put on your clothes. When you must walk, then walk. When you must sit, then sit. Don't have a single thought in your mind about seeking after Buddhahood. . . . If a man seeks the Buddha, then that man loses the Buddha. If you encounter the Buddha then slay him.' His expression was blunt and precisely to the point. Any self-conscious devotion to Buddha, any striving after enlightenment in an affected manner, only moved one further from one's ambition. It was 'like riding an ox in search of the ox'.* A forced effort in a particular direction was inviting the inevitable reaction in the opposite direction. The way of Zen, like the Tao of Lao-Tzu, though 'blurred and indistinct' could be sharp and clear. Its principle was spontaneity and intuition; it had no use for argument and intellect. 'Cut out sagacity; discard knowingness and the people will benefit an hundredfold', the Tao Te Ching had declared, and such is the spirit of Zen, which is easily misinterpreted as nihilistic and irrational.

Daily life in the Zen monastery usually begins with the monks reciting a sutra,† which they also repeat before meals. They proclaim,

Thus, Sariputra, all things have the character of emptiness, they have no beginning, no end, they are faultless and not faultless, they are not perfect and not imperfect. Therefore, O Sariputra, here in this emptiness there is no form, no perception, no name, no concepts, no Knowledge.

The sutra announces a negation of concepts. It is the concept of knowledge or ignorance that Zen denies. It even denies the sutra itself, for Lin Chi declared that sutras were no more than waste paper. Zen has no need for logic or rationale; jumping the boundaries of the concept, its spirit is most positive. It lies not in ideas, but in experience.

Doko, a philosopher, visited a Zen master,

'With what frame of mind should one discipline oneself in the truth?'

* See Alan Watts: *The Way of Zen*.

† Prajnaparamita-Hridaya Sutra: See D. T. Suzuki: *Introduction to Zen Buddhism*.

Said the Zen master, 'There is no mind to be framed, nor is there any truth in which to be disciplined.'

'If there is no mind to be framed and no truth in which to be disciplined, why do you have a daily gathering of monks who are studying Zen and disciplining themselves in the truth?'

The master replied: 'I have not an inch of space to spare, and where could I have a gathering of monks? I have no tongue, and how would it be possible for me to advise others to come to me?'

The philosopher then exclaimed, 'How can you tell me a lie like that to my face?'

'When I have no tongue to advise others, is it possible for me to tell a lie?'

Said Doko despairingly, 'I cannot follow your reasoning.'

'Neither do I understand myself,' concluded the Zen master.*

The master was neither indulging in negativity for its own sake, nor in word games in order to ridicule the philosopher. He was freeing the philosopher from the limited framework of reason in which he was trapped, in the process clearly pointing out that he himself did not 'understand', lest the philosopher continued to impose reason on the illogic of the dialogue. The master does not attempt to 'understand', for 'understanding' involves manipulating abstracts, and abstracts draw one away from experience.

The 'mondo', the questions and answers between disciple and master, are characterised by denials; the 'gatha', the sayings of the master, and the 'koan', the riddles posed by the master, are characterised by contradictions. These denials and contradictions involve a process of a stripping away of the concepts of experience until the moment when the disciple encounters the experience directly; he then has no further need of the concept. He can step outside logical dualism, the 'either/or' dichotomy of 'yes' or 'no', black or white, them or us, controller or controlled, and realise the indiscerptibility of the opposites. At such a moment the ability to identify with the immediate is fulfilled. The distinction between 'outside' and 'inside' is removed and he becomes one with his surroundings.

* See D. T. Suzuki: *Introduction to Zen Buddhism*, p. 57.

To illustrate this experience you can consider visual perception to be a dynamic process which is an interaction between an object and a viewer. At the moment of identity, the barrier between object and viewer is removed; they then exist not as separate entities, but by virtue of each other as inseparable parts of a common activity.

The concept must be denied in order to realise the experience itself, in the same way as the picture must be reduced in order to reveal the raw image. Logic is contrary to the spirit of Zen, for it dictates a pattern of thought and it supposes laws which impart a degree of self-consciousness. Once freed from logic, you perform effortlessly, without deliberation.

He who deliberates and moves his brush intent on making a picture, misses to a still greater extent the art of painting. Draw bamboos for ten years, become a bamboo then forget all about bamboos. ... (George Duthuit: *Chinese Mysticism and Modern Painting*.)

Freedom was obtained by the very discipline of Zen, which provides no licence for indulgence under the pretext of spontaneity or instinctive response; the discipline is rigorous. The point of awakening, sartori, came not as a result of forced conflict or struggle, but in a sudden moment of spontaneous clarity. The discipline led one to a stage from which it was possible to experience such a moment. The resulting 'enlightenment' was both a pinnacle of detachment from the 'snares of the world'— the ties of one's conditioned behaviour and responses, but it also simultaneously claimed a deep attachment to matter and Nature; it contained the seed of identity— to paint bamboo, it was necessary to become bamboo.

The implications of such an awakening were far-reaching. It undermined the foundations of the conventional religious experience and denied the validity of any system, political, social or religious, even its own peculiar system, though in so doing it reaffirmed a level of experience that transcended common blinkered perception. The identity that was found and its resulting freedom removed all sense of subordination of the individual, not only to artificial systems and conceptualised ideals, but also to Nature. There was no fear of Nature, so no need to fight it or to conquer it—one

[57]

would be fighting oneself. Likewise spiritual experience was no longer achieved by metaphorically prostrating oneself before the altar or in worship before the great idol. (The practice of Zen is not, however, devoid of sacrifice, for the act of self-sacrifice has been performed by the Japanese with an ease that is profoundly disturbing to many Westerners.) The spirit of Zen lay not in the devotions in the temple, but it could be found by watching the movement of the clouds, the flow of water, or the passing season.

Zen fell like a seed on to the fertile ground of Japan, for the native Shinto tradition realised the vitality of matter. Preserving archaic values, it had designated the tree, the mountain, the crag, the rock and the sea as dwelling-places of the spirits, hung prayers around stones of powerful shape and made wood into shrines of strikingly pure architectural form. Zen brought the focus of attention still closer to these elements. The elusive spirit could be expressed far more clearly and directly with stone, wood and earth than in any scripture. The spirit was omnipresent, it dwelt in the mountain and the pebble, it rode on the wind, it was carried by the stream. The gardener could contain it, for he realised the mountain through the rock, the forest through the moss and the ocean in the sand.

The painter Tsung Ping said that he could 'capture the beauty of Mount Sung and Mount Hua, the very mystery of the dark spirit of the universe, within a single picture' (see Ch. 3, p. 27). When Zen pervaded the art of the Muromachi Japan, the process of reduction was accelerated. The image of the landscape painter acquired a depth far beyond the representational; its scale became literally cosmic. Likewise the physical boundaries of the garden were reduced, its area became smaller, its images sharper and their intensity greater by virtue of the very simplicity and concentration of the design. As the physical space was reduced, the vision of space, or the illusion, expanded, and as the image moved from representation to abstraction, the potential of the image moved into previously unexpressed levels of experience.

With a single picture, both painter and gardener could capture the spirit as it moved. The design of the garden demanded that you approach it like a painting, or a painted scroll that had been unrolled before you.

The point from which you projected yourself into the picture was not the hypothetical point suspended in mid-air, as was necessary to conceive the complete mandala of the early gardens of paradise. You approached the garden like the conventional painting of the mandala, from a fixed point of rest, and this was of great importance.

Under the influence of Sung art, Japanese painters of the Muromachi period expressed their sense of identity with the Natural world in landscape paintings of unprecedented power, in which a mood of calm prevailed. Their field of vision was on a grandiose scale; huge mountains pierced the distant sky of these landscapes. The enveloping mist that characteristically wraps itself around the mountains of the pictures, softens the sharp crag and the rugged outline, and it also draws together the features of the paintings. Using a monochrome technique of charcoal ink applied with a soft brush and only faint tints of colour, light washes could be obtained and outlines could merge into the background. Faintly-defined cloud fades into space and the mist hides any distinctions between mountain, sky and water. The areas of the paintings that are untouched provide the very depth of the image; the space of the paintings extends like the endless sky.

I have found a similar experience to that of these paintings, when at home in the early morning I have looked across from a hilltop to nearby hills and down to the plain below. On some mornings just after dawn, I have reached the crest of the hill to find the plain spreading like a still, grey sea as the cloud lies beneath the surrounding hills. The nearer hills appear as some wild coastline; the further hills acquire an impressive new scale; they rise like a great mountain range at an inestimable distance. The point where the cloud-covered plain meets the sky cannot be distinguished, it is as if the still sea spreads out into a huge ocean. No horizon is defined and the space is immeasurable.

The tradition of these paintings is said to be 'as distinctive a contribution to art history as the ideal proportions with which the Greeks represented the physique of man'.* The Western classical tradition reinforces the

*Robert Paine; see Paine and Soper: *The Art and Architecture of Japan*, 1955.

view of man as the outsider looking on with calculated intellect, learning to control the elements and to master Nature; it is understandable therefore that his highest aspirations should be expressed in the cult of the human body, for man himself was seen as the active element and the instrument of change. How obvious then that the oriental imagination which gauged the flow of time by the changing season, should be stirred by landscape, and a landscape that revealed a vast panorama containing the extremes of the natural world—the jagged, thrusting rock and the subdued delicacy of the floating mist.

The cloud itself emphasises the transience of natural beauty, for it moves first veiling then revealing features; one can look at the landscapes of the Muromachi painters as if a fleeting moment had been caught, and the form of a mountain suddenly exposed behind the curtain of mist, only to be covered again. The scale of these panoramas had been achieved by the restraint of the painters. The art had become so highly developed, and the picture so reduced, that a whole mountain range could be painted in a few brush strokes. To attempt to represent the spirit would be to lose it; only by suggestion could it be captured. These paintings were not devoid of human figures, but where they do appear, they are small and inconspicuous, integral parts of the surrounding grandeur and never the focus of the picture. The oriental imagination immersed itself in landscape and through the landscape the human identity was not stifled—it was realised.

The greatest painter of the fifteenth century was Sesshu Toyo (1420–1506). He had entered Sokokuji temple in Kyoto and served under the Zen master, Shurin Suto; he then moved to Yamaguchi in the south-west of Honshu and came under the patronage of the Ouchi family, who had trading links with China. He reached China in 1467 in search of a painting master, but was disappointed. The Chinese, however, were greatly impressed by his work. He visited Zen monasteries in the south of China and the Ming capital, Peking, in the north, but the grandeur of the continental landscape, to which he was exposed, provided the greatest inspiration.

On his return to Japan in 1469 he avoided the capital,

where the Onin war was raging, and moved around northern Kyushu, eventually settling and establishing a studio in Oita. Between 1481 and 1484 he travelled all over Japan, drawing the landscape as he moved, then finally returned to Yamaguchi. The existing records of his life reveal a restless, inquisitive personality; his pilgrimages out into the wild beauty of Japan are evidence that his feeling for landscape was born out of experience, not from fantasy. His paintings were an expression of an individual in touch with the pulse of the land; his final inspiration was in his native roots.

Two paintings in particular reveal the characteristics of his style, the Autumn and the Winter Landscapes that are in the Tokyo National Museum. The foreground of both is composed of rocks, drawn with bold diagonal brush strokes. A path winds across the pictures towards the roofs of distant temples. Mountains rise steeply in

the background. The eye is drawn along the path, bordered by the sharp edges of stone, and off into the distant haze; one is guided out into space. The rocks of the foreground emerge with a rough solidity, infused with the strident personality of the artist. If the skill of the artist lay in the selection of the natural feature, allowing nature 'to reveal its intrinsic being', in so doing he demonstrated his own identity.

Like many of his painter contemporaries, Sesshu also designed gardens. Ten gardens in the Yama Guchi area and northern Kyushu have been attributed to him, though there is no definite proof that they are his work. However, the finest of the existing gardens, that of Joei-ji in Yama Guchi, originally belonged to Sesshu's patrons, the Ouchi family, and it displays characteristics of the painter's style. A lawn spreads from the verandah of the temple to the edge of a lake, which is surrounded on three sides by hills. The lawn is covered with numerous groups of stones and pruned shrubs. These outcrops of rocks standing in the grass have strong lines reminiscent of Sesshu's paintings—the flat tops and sharp diagonal edges. Possible influences on the design can be traced to the natural rock formations around Yama Guchi and northern Kyushu: at Hiraodai, near Fukuoka, and at Akiyoshidai in Yama Guchi Prefecture, the slopes of the hillside are dotted with rock; stones jut out from the meadowland in a landscape most uncommon in Japan. Many of the garden rock groupings are labelled after famous mountains, and the islands in the lake are named after the Chinese mystic isles. It is the stonework that bears the stamp of Sesshu and it is with the art of stones that the great Muromachi gardeners expressed the abstractions of landscape, laying their rocks as islands on the sand or mountains above the clouds.

On the outskirts of Kyoto is the temple of Ryoanji. Originally the site of a villa, in 1473 it was converted to a Zen temple by a military leader, Hosokawa Katsumoto, a powerful general in the Ashikaga government. The first temple was destroyed in the Onin war, but it was rebuilt by Katsumoto's son, Masamoto, in 1488. It is assumed that the garden of the existing temple was laid out during that reconstruction. The temple nestles among the lower, forested slopes of the mountains. A small pond, Oshidori, said to be a thousand years old, lies below the buildings. It was once filled with mandarin ducks; its banks are lined with trees and a bridge links the shore to one of three islands.

The first time I visited the temple, I went in the early morning, at a time when I hoped it would be quietest. It had been raining, the sky was overcast, but a stillness was in the air, like the calm after a storm. I followed a gravel path around the lake, crossed a narrow bridge and climbed the steps to the temple above, with its high roof curving as steeply as the slope of the mountains behind. Once within the temple complex, I walked out on to the polished wooden verandah, which ran alongside the rooms of the abbot. The sliding screen partitions were drawn fully open; the barriers between outside and inside were down.

The verandah faces a rectangular area, about twenty-five yards long and ten yards wide, which is enclosed on three sides by a wall, stained and mottled with age. The wall is made of clay and oil of rape seed, and is roofed with the customary heavy, grey tiles. Within the rectangular area are fifteen stones, which lie as if scattered in five groups on a background of coarse, grey sand. The sand is raked in circular patterns around the groups of stones, and in straight, shallow furrows over the remaining surface. There are no plants except for some moss at the base of the stones. There is a balance of forms between and within each group of stones.

The verandah is raised slightly above the ground and immediately beneath it is a border of round, black pebbles. After the rain the sand was a rich, dark colour, moisture hung from the leaves of the surrounding trees, water from the eaves splashed on the pebbles. The atmosphere was meditative.

During Tokugawa times the garden was called 'The Garden of Crossing Tiger Cubs'. This symbolised a Confucian moral of the good ruler protecting his country. But any symbolical analysis misses the vision of an awareness that is far more intuitive. As Matsukura, the Abbot of Ryoanji, said, the garden might better be called 'The Garden of Nothingness' (Mu-tei) or 'The Garden of Emptiness' (Ku-tei) than 'The Garden of Stones' (Seki-tei).

I was alone with the garden. My first reaction was to sit and collect myself. It was tempting to pace the verandah, to stoop and examine what lay before me from innumerable different angles, but there would be time for that later. Someone whose eye was trained to select patterns might have found the situation overwhelming; however, the patterns were striking not because they were in any way obtrusive, but because they emanated calm. The basis of the Zen discipline is the practice of meditation, zazen, which involves literally emptying the mind. The gardens, which were infused with the Zen spirit, were designed to be experienced from a position in which the viewer himself was as balanced as the arrangement before him. Such a position was a seated point of rest; you were not required to move out into the garden—it could be viewed as a complete image from the point of your own equilibrium.

Two hundred years before Ryoanji the cult of Amida had fostered the hope for some future salvation in the Pure Land of the West. The earlier gardens inspired by the Pure Land sought to reproduce the image of the idealised paradise. The imagination had been focused on the future, the fantasy had been nurtured and to see the garden as a complete image, one had to explore the dream. Zen had shifted the imagination from this preoccupation with the future, back to an awareness of the moment and the immediate. The garden, with its inherent balance, guided you to that point of equilibrium, when the sense of moment was captured.

Within the space of the garden, framed by the wall, images are compressed that extend from a view of landscape that is cosmic, to a pinpoint focus on matter which is microscopic. You can refer immediately to the native landscape that is reflected—the rocks stand like the rugged islands in the waves of an ocean, an image so familiar after the native coastline; or they rise with the thrusting volcanic rhythm of the mountains, the sand swirling around their base like cloud lingering on the lower slopes. The garden encompasses the depth of vision, the sense of space and the grandeur of scale that was explored by the painters, but by virtue of its abstract form, it offers further experience. As the eye closes in from the panorama and the illusory horizon is reduced,

[64]

the wave-like patterns of the sand flow with the force of the current rushing against the stepping-stones of a river. When you concentrate further on this wave-like motion, the raw image itself is revealed. The ripples of the sand flow as patterns of energy, as lines of force on some molecular scale, polarised around the stones. The wave motion is itself the fundamental image, rising and falling, but never actually moving, only appearing to move.

Unlike we Westerners, who count our achievements against the measure of time, the oriental vision saw time flow by with the ever-changing season and realised linear movement as only an illusion; the cycle always returned to the source. This was the constancy that contained the human identity. Man, buffeted and stroked by the waves of experience, developed and died, but beneath all that movement there was a factor that never changed, the centre of his 'being'—his 'self' ... All this has been achieved with a simplicity that we in the West might interpret as austerity.

The asymmetrical arrangement of the stones yields a vital harmony, but to dissect the groups and attempt to analyse the contrasts they contain, would be to deny the spirit with which the garden was created. The design was born not from a calculating sense of appropriate balance, but from a feeling for space, texture and rock, that had its origins in a more instinctive knowledge. It can be clearly understood that the arrangement of the stones was an art, and as such it would employ specific techniques. The asymmetry itself was revealing, for there was an odd number of groups and within each group there was an odd number of stones; by means of a technique known as 'hacho', which meant 'breaking the harmony', the actual balance was obtained.

[65]

Zen had cut through the social strata. Devoid of the symbolism of Esoteric Buddhism, the Zen-inspired art was accessible to those outside government circles and the higher levels of the social hierarchy. The Zen temples moved in the opposite direction to the Esoteric sects, who often criticised the unconventional behaviour of the Zen adepts, and the Zen temples patronised social outcasts. In medieval Japan there were four distinct classes: samurai, merchants, farmers and artisans. But like the Indian caste system there was a sector of society who were considered 'untouchables'. (The origins of this class may in fact lie in the Indian system, which could have been introduced by the early Buddhist missionaries.) Their ancestors were said to be vagabonds and thieves. The untouchables were suitable for the impure work of slaughter, tanning or clearing the drains. They were once referred to as 'hinin' or nonhumans. (Today a million of these 'untouchables', known as 'burakumin', still live in isolated enclaves in Japan.)

In fifteenth-century Kyoto they were known as 'Kawaramono', meaning 'river-bank' people in reference to the slum area where they lived. These kawaramono often worked in the temple gardens and in time became garden designers. One of Yoshimasa's famous gardeners was a kawaramono called Zen'ami, who had a high reputation for his skilled stonework. On the back of one of the stones at Ryoanji is an inscription of two signatures, Kotaro and Seijiro. Research has revealed that these men were kawaramono working in Kyoto gardens at the end of the fifteenth century. Perhaps the purest and most powerful of all the gardens was shaped by the hands of men who had been regarded as so impure that they were not even human.

The kawaramono probably laid the stones under the direction of Soami (?–1525), a tea master and painter, to whom is attributed the actual design of the garden. Soami came from a line of painters all of whom employed the wash technique that had been developed by Sesshu. Noami (1397–1471), the grandfather of Soami, had been an attendant to the shogun and had catalogued the shogun's collection of Chinese paintings; he was considered the leading authority of his time. His son Geiami (1431–1485) also had a high reputation as a painter. Soami, the third painter in the extraordinary family line, had been patronised by Yoshimasa and his name is often linked with the garden of Ginkakuji. He completed his grandfather's catalogue, 'Kundai-kan socho-ki' (Notebook of the Shogun's Art Secretary), which was a most authoritative survey of Chinese art, and was himself highly regarded as an artist. Ironically, though this family worked in the Zen temples, at one time they were certainly Amidists, as 'Ami', the suffix of their names, suggests.

Soami's talents were diverse and his garden skill was not confined to the use of stone and sand. By using moss he created another form of dry landscape, which also contained the image of water. In a quiet, secluded corner of the great temple complex of Daitokuji in Kyoto is the small Zen temple, Ryogen-in. The original meditation hall, hojo, which was built in 1502, still stands. Beside the verandah of the hall is the garden of Ryogintei. Again a wall, roofed with tiles, encloses a rectangular space and pebbles border the edge nearest the verandah. The area is even smaller than the garden of Ryoanji. The surface is covered with gently undulating moss. A few stones lie embedded in the moss; azaleas, which have been cut very low, grow around the base of several rocks. About half-way along the garden, a tall flat-topped stone protrudes close to the far wall. This stone is said to represent Shumisen, the core of the universe.

The scale of Soami's moss garden, like that of Ryoanji, could be seen as a huge panorama. Ryogintei has been referred to as an image of the ocean, the waves of the moss gently lapping the rocky islands. But the expanse of green moss immediately struck me in a different way from the other dry landscapes that I had seen. It was certainly an extensive panorama, broken by the towering mountains, but the moss slopes had the texture of the thickly-forested hillsides of Japan. I changed my focus to the detail of the moss immediately below me. Its fine needle structure arranged around the stem was the image of a tree, like the tall Japanese cryptomeria, sugi (*Cryptomeria japonica*), which grows in the forests of the hills surrounding Kyoto.

Just as the Amidists projected the image of the paradise mandala from the point in space, the Zen garden

in circular ripples around it. The stone floated in the pool of sand. In the background was a well; the element of water was all around, though nowhere in Ryogen-in is there a stream or cascade. The image of the sea was right there in the sand.

Also within the precincts of Daitokuji is another small Zen temple, Daisen-in, founded by the priest Kogaku in 1513. The abbot's study faces a garden which is about fifteen yards long and only three yards wide, at the back of which runs a long, white, plastered wall. The study itself is decorated with sliding panels on which Soami painted a magnificent set of landscapes. The design of the garden is traditionally attributed to Soami, though it could also have been the work of the founder himself. When you are seated by the edge of the room, the garden flows from left to right (north to south). In the left-hand corner are some tall rocks and small trees, which despite their size fit perfectly into the scale of the area. The source of the motion is in these rocks; it is as if a great cascade plunges to a torrent below. The sand at the foot of the stones is raked into a swirling eddy of patterns.

The tall, upright forms are balanced by a single horizontal slab of rock, that traverses the sand like a natural bridge over the rushing stream. As you follow the current, you see pointed rocks that border the sand like a deep mountain valley. The garden is divided by a wooden bridge, which spans the sand and forms a walled partition. In the middle of the partition is a cusped window, Kato mado, which frames a view of the tall rocks of the cascade. Beyond the bridge the sand opens out from a stream into the mouth of a great river. An extraordinary boat-shaped stone points in the direction of the current. At the far end of the garden, the patterns in the sand curve under the verandah itself and disappear from sight. The sand flows out into the sea.

of Soami with its detailed focus on Nature also contained an image that we today might find in flight— a view that was aerial; it was a bird's-eye panorama that could compress a hundred miles into a single foot.*

Later I turned and followed the verandah of the meditation hall. Where the verandah linked the building with the rest of the temple complex was a still smaller garden only a few feet wide. At one end of the rectangle was a single upright stone; at the other end there were two. A low, flat stone lay on the sand, which spread

* Tessen Soki, 'Ka Senzui no Fu'; 'reducing thirty thousand miles to the distance of a single foot'. See Teiji Itoh: *The Japanese Garden: An Approach to Nature*.

The Way of Tea

The art of Cha-no-yu consists of nothing else but boiling water, making tea and sipping it.

Sen no Rikyu

While the roji is meant to be a passageway
Altogether outside this earthly life
How is it that people only contrive
To sprinkle it with the dust of the mind.

Sen no Rikyu

The most powerful form, one that could suggest the transience of Nature or the movement of the 'Dark Spirit', and in the process display vitality, was achieved by simplification. The artist uncovered the pure image by divesting the picture of the superfluous and exploring the space of the image. The discipline of Zen had encouraged such a process.

Simplicity characterised not only the garden, the painting, the building or an attitude, it also characterised a level of experience in which one moved and responded effortlessly yet precisely, with a heightened awareness of flow and natural rhythm, senses alert, mind calm and body relaxed. Such a performance was a ritual with the conventions peculiar to a ritual, yet devoid of rigid formality. As the gardener cultivated the purity of form, the master of the ritual cultivated grace. As the garden created space into which you could project yourself, the ritual created detachment in which you could face yourself. The performance displayed sensibility in balance, form and contrast—it required a visual appreciation, a feel for texture and sensitivity to sound. The garden had a most important function in guiding the eye to appreciate the performance. This ritual is called an art—the art of tea, Cha-no-yu.

The best tea leaves must have 'creases like the leathern boot of Tartar horsemen, curl like the dewlap of a mighty bullock, unfold like a mist rising out of a ravine, gleam like a lake touched by a Zephyr, and be wet and soft like fine earth newly swept by rain'.* So wrote Lu Wu (d. A.D. 804), a tea master in China during the T'ang dynasty, and author of the first book on tea, the Ch'a Ching, the Holy Scripture of Tea. Tea had been a plant valued for its medicinal qualities and brewed as a

* See K. Okakura: *The Book of Tea.*

beverage by the inhabitants of the valley of the Yangtse-Kiang since the fourth century. By the T'ang dynasty the properties of the plant and the preparation of the beverage had evidently been assumed to have spiritual connotations; Buddhist monks used it to counter sleep during meditation, and the Taoists claimed it was an ingredient in the elixir of immortality.

Lu Wu had described the poetry of tea and saw the harmony of Buddhist and Taoist symbolism reflected in its preparation. During the Sung dynasty the appreciation for the beverage had turned into a cult; rare teas were prized and tasting tournaments were held. But the spiritual associations of the cult were taken a stage further than the symbolism of Lu Wu, for the preparation of the tea not only represented Taoist concepts of change, it was a manifestation of change itself; it became more than the vital image of change, it was the enactment of the Taoist way. The Zen (Ch'an) sects of southern China later incorporated the Taoist spirit into a profound ritual.

In the Sung dynasty the actual preparation also changed; the leaves were first ground into a powder, the water added and the liquid briskly stirred with a finely-split bamboo whisk. This was the method of preparation which was adopted by the Japanese in Cha-no-yu. The tea plant was introduced to Japan from China by the Zen master Eisai (1141–1215); the ritual was introduced about fifty years later by the monk Dai-o. Shuko, who conducted the tea ceremony for Yoshimasa at the Togudo in Ginkakuji (see Ch. 5, p. 51), incorporated the ceremony into the Japanese aesthetic tradition, and is considered the founder of Cha-no-yu.

The origins of the ritual lie in Taoism, and its development is strongly linked with the spirit and practice of Zen. The various characteristics of the Japanese sensibility were all assimilated in this ceremony; the contrasting elements of the Japanese imagination were crystallised in the one act, in which the mind was purified and the senses sharpened.

The tea cult has been invested with religious overtones, and has often been compared to the use of the sacramental wine in the Communion. The mood of Cha-no-yu is one of quiet introspection, aided by the calming effect of the tea, in contrast to the more extroverted, jovial associations of wine. Though it cannot be considered as a religious rite in the conventional sense of 'religious', Cha-no-yu has strong spiritual significance. The four and a half tatami of the tea room at the Togudo, and the bare simplicity of the later tea houses can hardly be considered as suitable for communal religious experience. However, the atmosphere that was cultivated was conducive to a serene tranquillity. Against a background that was unobtrusive in the extreme, the senses were guided to focus on sounds and forms that were emphasised by the very restraint of their surroundings.

Though the ritual was a social activity, one of brotherhood, devoid of social barriers—a point where people from different sectors of society might meet—the feeling associated with the ritual was one of solitude and detachment. Again, in the true spirit of Zen, the ritual also claimed a deep attachment to Nature. If the mood of the ritual was not attuned to the flow of Nature, it was empty. The Zen master Takuan (1573–1645) said,

The way of Cha-no-yu, therefore, is to appreciate the spirit of a naturally harmonious blending of Heaven and Earth, to see the pervading presence of the five elements (wu-hsing) by one's fireside, where the mountains, rivers, rocks and trees are found as they are in Nature, to draw the refreshing water from the well of Nature, to taste with one's own mouth the flavour supplied by Nature. How grand this enjoyment of the harmonious blending of Heaven and Earth.★

The mood of the ceremony can best be illustrated by the four underlying principles, Harmony (wa), Reverence (kei), Purity (sei) and Tranquillity (jaku). Harmony indicates balance, the principle on which the oriental attitude is pivoted; the balance of the opposite elements is the image of natural order. The Taoists sought the balance of Heaven and Earth, as did the early diviners with the Book of Changes. Takuan had likewise seen the balance of Cha-no-yu in the 'harmonious blending of heaven and earth'. According to Daisetz Suzuki,★ the character 'wa', 和, meaning harmony, can also be translated as 'yawaragi', meaning

★ See D. T. Suzuki: *Zen and Japanese Culture.*

'gentleness of spirit' and gentleness is the implication of 'wa'. The gentle is the unobtrusive, the powerful yet subtle and restrained. Gentleness contains the secret of suggestion; to be gentle is not to be conspicuously demonstrative, but to reveal without forcefulness, to capture the spirit by what one omitted, rather than by what one represented. So gentleness pervades the landscapes of Sesshu as it does the gardens of Soami. Every detail of the tea house and its garden, the ritual and the utensils reflect gentleness, like the gentleness of the landscape, of the mist on the mountain. Personal gentleness of spirit was demonstrated in the gestures with which the ritual was performed.

Reverence (kei) refers to an attitude achieved by gentleness; its implications are social. To obtain harmony, the individual refrains from placing himself above others. To be sensitive to the natural elements you do not subordinate Nature—to do so would be to detach yourself from the natural flow. Similarly the way of Cha-no-yu is one of humility. The tea house and garden are small and simple and in no way ostentatious. To enter the house, you stoop under a low doorway as a gesture of humility. The Zen masters recognised the humble mind as the most receptive.

Purity (sei) is the natural image itself, devoid of the superficial. It is the experience, not the concept. Purity is a characteristic of the Shinto tradition (the transfer of the ancient capital after the death of the Emperor was carried out to avoid impurity). It is emphasised in Shinto ritual and reflected in Shinto architecture; the timbers of the shrine at Ise were blessed and purified before use; the carpenters were purified before they began work on the shrine. The overt simplicity of the building expressed the purity; purity was the feeling for texture and the grain of wood in its natural state, or for the rough and jagged shapes of uncut stone.

The tea house was the paragon of purity—a room of extreme simplicity, in which no materials other than the natural textures of wood, earth and stone were evident. It was immaculately clean. The dust of the room had to be swept away, as, in the words of the Zen masters, you wiped away 'the dust of the mind'. Purity was not, however, a category of spiritual hygiene. The pure form

★ See D. T. Suzuki: *Zen and Japanese Culture.*

as they go through the transformation of seasons, appearing and disappearing, blooming and withering. As visitors are greeted here with due reverence, we listen quietly to the boiling water in the kettle, which sounds like a breeze passing through the pine needles, and become oblivious of all worldly woes and worries; we then pour a dipperful of water from the kettle, reminding us of the mountain stream, and thereby our mental dust is wiped off.'

The ritual was a means to purity. For a moment one could feel like Han Shan, returning to the slopes of Cold Mountain, who said,

> Today I'm back at Cold Mountain
> I'll sleep by the creek and purify my ears.

The final principle, Tranquillity (jaku), is perhaps the most elusive yet the most fundamental. It suggests two qualities displayed in Cha-no-yu, 'wabi' and 'sabi'. Both imply simplicity and solitude. 'Sabi' is applied more to individual objects, 'wabi' to a way of life. Both involve an appreciation for things suggestive of old age and decay. In contrast to our Western sense of beauty, which is concentrated on the feelings associated with the warmth and growth of spring, the Japanese also realise the beauty of the gnarled and twisted form of the dead tree and the potency of the autumnal mood (see Ch. 1).

In the natural cycle, the death force is inseparable from the life force; beauty is in those elements which depict the flow, whether they are flourishing or decaying. An object displays 'sabi' when it is simple and unpretentious, or when it is old, worn and polished through use. A simple peasant rice bowl might possess more 'sabi' than the finest tea bowl. 'Wabi' and 'sabi' epitomise the art of understatement so precious to the Japanese sensibility.

Outside the tea room of Sen no Rikyu there was a bed of morning glory in full flower. The shogun, Hideyoshi, hearing of their beauty, announced his desire to see their magnificent bloom. When he arrived there were no flowers to be seen, but on entering the tea room, a single morning glory was displayed in a vase. The beauty of the flower could be fully witnessed in the solitary spray; by restrained understatement and

was that which revealed the image of the natural elements most clearly; the dust is swept away so that the full beauty of the grain of the wood is exposed. The garden of the tea house is likewise kept meticulously, but if every fallen leaf was swept aside, the atmosphere would be artificial and sterile.

The great tea master, Sen no Rikyu (1521–1591), when cleaning the garden path, would sweep it until there was no dust, then shake a tree so that a few leaves fell to the ground; the garden was then more natural and closer to purity. Cha-no-yu was a purifying ritual; the senses were stimulated to perceive the inherent harmony of the natural world, by such simple images as the grain of the wood, the glaze on a cup or the sound of bubbling water.

Takuan said '. . . in this room we can enjoy the streams and rocks as we do the rivers and mountains in Nature, and appreciate the various moods and sentiments suggested by the snow, the moon, and the trees and flowers, suggestion the eye could focus without distraction; it could accommodate the image completely.

In the eighth century, inspired by the vision of the T'ang poets, the nobility of Nara had found tranquillity away from the life of the capital, in the small, rustic retreat. It was necessary to step outside your worldly affairs and to become revitalised by the detachment that solitude offered. Alone on the mountainside, with your 'self' and the elements, you could merge into the world of Nature, unhampered by your social ties and desires; you could also discover the source of identity. While some found tranquillity in the monastery and the brotherhood of the monastic community, others found it in solitude.

Today in certain parts of Asia, there are those who are still making their solitary pilgrimages out into the wilderness. Some men succeeded in losing their 'selves' altogether. If they had sought a meaning to their existence by climbing the mountain, they would have lost all notion of meaning; they would have fused themselves with their surroundings and forgotten their desires. These men had no need to return from the mountain—they had already found the Way. Such men are few and their footsteps inconspicuous. Perhaps this is what Liu Ch'iu-Yin had meant (see Ch. 3, p. 29) when, describing Han Shan, he had said, 'Thus men who have made it hide their tracks.'

Most men came down off the mountain and back into their families, their work and the social structure, but they carried with them a certain knowledge, born out of the experience of solitude, and from time to time it was necessary to rediscover that tranquillity. In the eighth century the lonely retreat was an ideal, possibly even a fantasy, evoked by the imagery of the T'ang poets, or inspired by some Chinese landscape. However, it established a precedent which was absorbed into the very heart of the Japanese imagination. The tradition survived to find expression in the tranquillity of Cha-no-yu. This was the solitude of 'wabi', inseparable from the principle of tranquillity. It was the emotion contained in the ritual.

Withered leaves lie deep by the eaves, and moss has spread over the floor. . . . Only in a hut built for the moment can one live without fears. It is very small, but it holds a bed where I may lie at night and a seat for me in the day; it lacks nothing as a place for me to dwell. The hermit crab chooses to live in little shells because it well knows the size of its body. The osprey stands on deserted shores because it fears human beings. I am like them. Knowing myself and the world, I have no ambitions and do not mix in the world. I seek only tranquillity.

From Hojoki by Kamo no Chomei (1212)

The ideal of the tea house was a hut far off in the hills or by some deserted shoreline. When the house was built within a temple complex or on an estate, it was designed to suggest this ideal. In the modern house, the tea house might be replaced by a room in a separate wing of the house, or by a building in a quiet, secluded part of the garden.

The roof of the house is thatched, the walls are of dried clay. You enter through a low doorway. Inside, the floor is covered with tatami. In the centre of the room is a sunken pit, where an iron kettle is boiled over charcoal. The room is bare except for a small alcove (tokonoma); in the alcove hangs a scroll (kakemono), decorated with either a painting or calligraphy; beneath it, on a low shelf, there is a vase with a single spray of flowers and possibly an old incense burner. The light is soft and subdued through the paper screens, shoji. The utensils are kept in a small anteroom. Within the standard area of four and a half tatami, there is nothing superfluous. The wooden pillar of the alcove might be rough and irregular, and probably of a different wood from the other timber of the building; there is no repetition.

The guests enter quietly and sit the length of the room facing the kettle. The master, or the host, enters with the utensils, which he places by the brazier. Each movement and gesture that he makes is precise, but flowing with the grace and ease of apparent spontaneity. A small lacquer tea caddy, containing the powdered tea, is wiped then opened. Using a bamboo spoon the master places the tea in the tea bowl.

The bowl is the vessel that is passed and handled by all present. Like a precious treasure, it may be handed down over the centuries from generation to generation.

[75]

It can evoke a season, it can contain the power of 'sabi' in its feel and texture as in the colours of its glaze. Yet often its peculiar delicacy may lie in its rough irregularity; its glaze not dazzling, but evocative.

The Chinese had attempted to reproduce the quality of jade in their ceramics; in the south the blue glaze was characteristic, and in the north a white glaze. In the T'ang dynasty, when the tea was prepared from a solid cake form, the white glaze tinted the tea with pink, so the blue glaze was preferred. But during the Sung dynasty, when the powdered form was used, which was later adopted into Cha-no-yu, dark and heavy bowls were found to be the most suitable. The Japanese, with their sympathy for the rough qualities of peasant pottery, found this form most attractive. Again, symmetrical forms were avoided, the geometrical shape was too artificial. Perfection lay in the imperfect. The asymmetry of the house, the garden and the utensils might appear most conspicuous to the Western sense of proportion.

With a bamboo ladle, water is poured from a jug into the bowl. It is then stirred with the fine bamboo whisk. The tea is passed from guest to guest, and when empty the bowl is admired by the guests; later the other utensils might be passed among them. Little is said, other than comments admiring these utensils. However, the ritual is only an introduction. After the tea, the atmosphere is calm and silent, with only the sound of the water bubbling on the charcoal, and the faint scent of incense. Any comments that are made are appropriate to the mood. The mind is freed from distraction, anxiety and the fears and ambitions of worldly affairs. It is then most receptive. One is ready to sense 'the five elements by one's fireside, where the mountains, rivers, rocks and trees are found as they are in Nature'.

The tea garden (chaniwa) serves as an approach to the tea house. It marks the transition from the outside world to the detachment of the inner world of Cha-no-yu. It is arranged about a path known as the 'roji', a Buddhist term referring to the path to rebirth in the land of Purity and Tranquillity. As you walked along the roji, you severed your ties with the outer world, and moved closer to the calm and seclusion of the tea house. This

period of transition corresponded to the preliminary stages of meditation.

Unlike any of the previous gardens, there was no point along the path where it was intended that the garden be viewed as a complete composition. Its purpose was to create a mood but never to arrest one's attention. Its design was based on suggestion alone; its features provided no distraction. By the skilful use of 'wabi' and 'sabi' the atmosphere was set for the ritual that lay ahead. Since the garden began at the gate and ended at the tea house there was a sequence to its design; this sequential arrangement was later developed in the large stroll gardens of the Tokugawa period. Specific features that were introduced to the tea garden, such as the stepping-stones, the stone lanterns and the water basin, have survived to this day as common features in the modern, urban garden. As the ceremony had linked many features of the Japanese sensibility and affected the development of the aesthetic tradition, the tea garden made a great impression on the changing garden style.

The early tea gardens were almost completely bare so as to offer no possible distraction, but as the simplicity of the house itself was cultivated, the garden developed in contrast and shrubs, trees and stones were introduced. The construction of large, artificial mounds and mountains was impossible within the small area. Some tea masters considered that fencing was too artificial and they enclosed their gardens with hedges. Sen no Rikyu is said to have designed a garden for a temple near Osaka on the Inland Sea: the garden was surrounded by a double row of hedges, which emphasised its seclusion. When you stooped over the water basin, you could catch a glimpse of the sea between the hedges. From the pool of water your eye travelled to the ocean itself, framed or captured by the enclosure.

The plants in the garden were chosen to suggest a wild landscape, like the wilderness of a remote sea shore or a mountain trail, to complement the solitude of the house itself. There might be ferns around the stones, a maple tree for its autumn colour, which evoked the poignancy of the passing season, and the familiar form of the twisted pine tree. Flowers were avoided, for they reduced the effect of the few flowers arranged within the tea room.

[77]

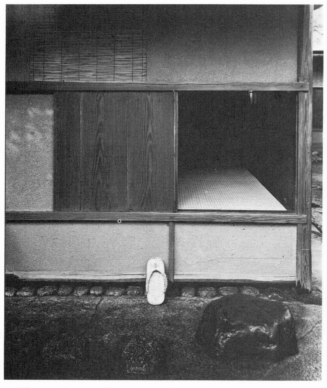 

The path was the key to the garden. The stepping-stones that constituted the path could hold the power of 'sabi'. Embedded in the moss, maybe surrounded with dried pine needles, they were arranged with all the art of asymmetry. The rough shapes of these flat-topped stones, placed at irregular intervals, drew one's concentration as one walked; you moved precisely, placing your feet with care. You were subtly drawn away from focusing on any possible image that the garden might present. The shrubs and trees around the path were only glimpsed, and so the mood of suggestion was maintained, the design not scrutinised. Your attention was drawn to your footsteps by virtue of the irregularity of the stones. When you reached the house, you were already moving with precision.

The Choandoki, a collection of anecdotes on Cha-no-yu, which was published in 1640, relates that the stepping-stones were originated by a tea master called Dotei, who was visited one day by Yoshimasa, on his way back from a hawking expedition. The path to Dotei's hut being muddy, Yoshimasa ordered his attendants to spread the ground with their paraphernalia, to allow him a clean passage. This sight inspired Dotei to lay the stones. Typical of Japanese taste, the beautiful was both functional and aesthetic.

The stone lantern is another example of such a combination. It was originally introduced to the garden to provide light when the ritual was held at night. The Heian gardens had been illuminated by bonfires, but bonfires would have been most inappropriate for the subdued atmosphere of the approach to the tea house. The lanterns which were used in the Buddhist temples, and as votive lights in the Shinto shrines, were considered ideal for the tea garden. When the tea cult was flourishing under Sen no Rikyu in the sixteenth century, there may have been many lanterns available from the ruins of the temples sacked during civil war. Such lanterns—old, weathered, patched with moss—would have been most in keeping with the cultivated mood of neglect and solitude in the garden, as they flickered among the trees and cast shadows over the stones.

The water basin likewise had functional origins; it was used for washing one's hands before entering the tea house. Its purpose was also symbolical: stooping over the low basin was a gesture of humility, and the washing anticipated the cleansing and purifying of the spirit that took place in the ritual that followed. The basin was formed from a hollowed piece of granite; sometimes its outer surfaces were left rough and uncut, but its inner bowl polished smooth as glass. The basin revealed the element of water, essential to the garden. Stooping over the small pool contained in the rock, which overflowed and splashed on to the slabs of moss-covered stone and dark pebbles at the foot of the basin, you might catch your own reflection in the mirror of the surface, framed in rock, and be reminded that it was more than your hands that were being purified.

Like the ritual, the tea garden embodied the art of the suggestive and the unobtrusive. It contained none of the scope of the abstractions of landscape, designed for contemplation; it was not viewed from the fixed position of balance; it represented only the point of transition. But beneath the exterior simplicity there was great subtlety and sophistication.

The gardens were designed by the tea masters themselves, and reflected the principles of their art—the beauty of the functional and the potency of understatement. The feeling expressed in such refined yet modest beauty was profoundly spiritual, and held the key to their identity. The beauty of the form would be hollow, the ritual empty, if the vision of the vital flow of Nature was not extended to an awareness that their own lives were inseparable from that cycle to which they were so sensitive.

For a century after the end of the Onin war in 1467, the country continued in an age of feudal turmoil, known as the Age of the Country at War. The frailty of life was a blatant fact of the day. Yet in the detachment that Cha-no-yu offered, transience was endowed with beauty, and was cultivated. If there was any meaning in the chaos of their times, it was contained in the flow. Indeed out of the violence of the sixteenth century, a new Japan was being built. Much of the power of the image of decay, the mood of 'wabi', lay in the future growth that it implied.

As has been stated, Cha-no-yu has been compared to the Communion, and the comparison, though often misleading, can be illuminating. The great master of the art, Sen no Rikyu, demonstrated that the grace of the performance represented not only an attitude to life, but a way of death. Sen no Rikyu was accused of a conspiracy against the shogun, Hideyoshi, and his end was inevitable. On his final day, he summoned his disciples to his last ceremony, which he performed calmly, with no trace of his intentions. After the ritual, he presented each disciple with one of the utensils, with the exception of the bowl, which he himself took and broke.

When his guests had left him, he removed his kimono, to reveal a white death robe. With a smile on his face and with the ease and detachment he had cultivated, he conducted the final rite of self-immolation.[*] The way of tea was a performance in which one could place one's life on the spinning continuum. When perfected it contained symbolism as powerful as that of the Last Supper, and again one could move or even die as effortlessly as the seasons pass or the moon rises.

I have referred to the practice of the art as a performance, because it involved not only a knowledge of Nature but an enactment of that knowledge. Throughout the ritual, the master moved with the developed skill of an actor, using his role to impart the beauty of the natural world. The author of the Noh theatre, Zeami Motokiyo (1363–1443), described a principle which was the ultimate achievement of the actor; it applied to all the Japanese arts alike. This principle was called 'yugen' and contained the mystery of suggestion. Zeami said that to experience 'yugen' was,

To watch the sun sink behind a flower-clad hill, to wander on and on in a huge forest with no thought of return, to stand upon the shore and gaze after a boat that goes hid by far-off islands, to ponder on the journey of wild geese seen and lost among the clouds.

Perhaps no culture so refined, has displayed such sympathy for a beauty so uncontrived.

[*] See K. Okakura: *The Book of Tea*, Boston, 1906.

The Garden Path

The architecture and garden of the tea house express a most refined simplicity. Subsequent designs reflected elements of this cultivated yet natural simplicity, which came to be known as 'sukiya', meaning 'artlessness'. The tradition represented in 'sukiya', with its origins in the primitive architectural style of Ise, was reduced and distilled to an almost perfect form through the cult of tea. There is a limit though to how far a tradition can be refined or an image reduced, without losing the original source of inspiration.

As the vision of the garden changed from a vast landscape park to a few stones on a sea of sand, the expression became more articulate, the picture closer to the raw image, the experience of landscape less artificial and more direct. The vision, though timeless, was a product of an age. Circumstances change, new influences are discovered, old inspiration is lost, and so too do visions change. The image of Ryoanji could accommodate no further development, the tea house and its garden could undergo no further simplification. The features of such gardens survived and passed through the familiar process of adoption—were imitated, absorbed, then reinterpreted. They were finally applied in contexts far removed from their origins, and assumed new functions.

As the garden itself inevitably changed, the old vision died and a new expression was made, which reflected a different attitude and mirrored the aspirations of a different time. As the garden reflected transience, it too grew and died. Maybe at a time when more than ever we are divorced from landscape and our very own nature, the garden will take on a new meaning. Perhaps it already has.

In the seventeenth century, the subtlety of the tea house style was transposed from the tea master's hut to an Imperial palace. The result was architecture of astounding elegance and classical simplicity, yet far removed from the small, remote cottage of Cha-no-yu. The Katsura estate lies outside Kyoto by the river of the same name. (Katsura is the Japanese Judas tree, *Circidiphyllum japonicum*; its associations are strongly lunar for allegedly it can be seen growing under moonlight.) The estate, situated in a vicinity that had been popular for country retreats since the Heian period, was the property of

[81]

Prince Toshihito (1579–1629), the younger brother of the Emperor Goyozei (1571–1617). The garden of the palace is traditionally attributed to Kobori Enshu, a famous landscape gardener of the early seventeenth century (his role is questioned by some modern authorities who believe the garden may have been designed by Toshihito himself).

In 1620, when Kobori was supposedly commissioned, he is said to have stipulated that there was to be no limit on expenditure, no one was to view the garden before completion and there was to be no time limit for the work; in four years it was finished. It was an elaborate undertaking; devoid of any of the religious connotations of the great paradise gardens, it was a purely aesthetic pursuit. Twenty years later, additional details were included in the garden and a main hall constructed by the Prince's son, Toshitada (1619–1662), in time for a visit by the retired Emperor Gomizunoo in 1658.

The approach to the palace is a long, straight avenue, bordered on either side by hedges and paved with small stones. The line of the avenue is formal and elegant in contrast to the narrow, irregular 'roji'. Like the Heian shinden style, the buildings are arranged so that each room could open out on to a garden or courtyard.

[82]

Garden and palace are integrated in the design as a whole. The numerous different views of the garden are framed by the buildings or the surrounding landscape.

Refined taste is demonstrated in every detail of the rooms; for example in the Miyukido, the main hall especially constructed for the Emperor's visit, even the fastenings that conceal the nail heads in the joinery, the Kugikakushi, are shaped like narcissi, and the shelves are made from ebony, sandalwood, betel palm and other rare woods. In contrast to the basic austerity of the tea house this refinement might appear as extravagance, but compared to other Imperial residences, adorned with gold and lacquer, it is most modest. The panels of the screens are painted in the soft hues and washes of the Muromachi artists. The rooms are light, uncluttered and spacious. Beside a pavilion there is a moon viewing platform, Furushoin, of bamboo which serves as a link between the building and the garden.

Around the garden there are several small pavilions and a tea house; they are simple thatched cottages built out of clay, bamboo and reeds. Characteristically, however, beneath the exterior simplicity and the exquisite taste, there is subtle design, for the eye is always led to discover the unexpected. The restraint of the tea house

had been adopted to fit a new convention, then applied with originality. The proportions of the rooms change suddenly, or you round a corner to find yet another view out on to the garden. It was the art of 'the seen and hidden', mie-gakure—the art of surprise.

Like the shinden mansions, the main buildings faced a great lake around which the garden was structured. The contours of the lake wind around small secluded bays; the banks turn to hide further views until one comes to a bend to be confronted suddenly by another unexpected scene. There are woods and hills, and islands joined by bridges; great rocks tower like huge cliff faces. The shores change from soft, green banks to stone walls; there is even a pebbled peninsula. But the key to the garden, through which the flexibility is maintained, is the garden path. The path with its meandering detours leads one into the subtlety of the garden. It changes all the time, from round stones embedded in moss, to narrow blocks of granite, to rough irregular stepping-stones or a rock and pebble pathway. It is the asymmetry of the 'roji' that has been transposed; just as the tea garden was structured around the path, so too is the stroll garden. The stone lanterns line the path as in the tea gardens, and numerous water basins are arranged around the tea house. Stepping-stones lead out into the water, and on the last stone is placed a ladle; there is no basin, there is the lake itself.

The buildings had assumed much of the simplicity of the tea house and the garden had adopted the features of the 'chaniwa'. The refinement appropriate to the Imperial family and the modesty and understatement of the tea masters had been combined in design of great beauty. The architecture was an assimilation of centuries of tradition reinterpreted with original and restrained vision.★ But what once held the seed of personal identity and could capture a dark, universal spirit as it moved, was rapidly being replaced by the decorative.

A detailed knowledge of the Tale of Genji was necessary in order to appreciate the illusions suggested by

★ The Japanese architect Kenzo Tange has traced the influence of the ancient cultures of Jommon and Yayoi in the architecture of Katsura. See Kenzo Tange: *Katsura: Tradition and Creation in Japanese Architecture*, Yale University Press, London and New Haven, 1960.

[85]

many of the views. The novel, Toshihito's favourite book, had been the source of inspiration; the full subtlety could only be appreciated by those well acquainted with it. The garden was designed for a prince and it can therefore be assumed that those around him, his entourage, would have been familiar with the book. How different though from the timeless vision and depth of experience contained at Ryoanji. The garden was the recreation of a literary illusion and had been cultivated in seclusion for the court. The garden was moving away from the sense of moment, the directness of the Zen influence, and the image of landscape itself, back to the fantasy and its accompanying extravagance.

The military ruler, Hideyoshi, died at the end of the sixteenth century. The period of internal strife came to a close. The last of Hideyoshi's family and retainers were defeated at the siege of Osaka castle in 1615, by the general's former deputy, Tokugawa Ieyasu. It was a

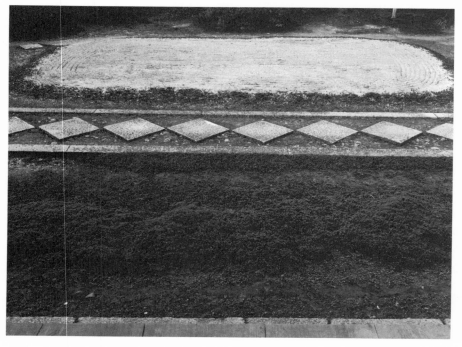

turning point in Japanese history. At last Japan entered a period of stability under the Tokugawa family; it was to last for two and a half centuries, but was achieved at a cost.

Ieyasu assumed the title of shogun and established his capital at his military seat at Edo, a fishing village, which is now modern Tokyo. To maintain political control over the feudal lords, the daimyo, a system known as 'alternating in attendance', Sankin Kotai, was introduced. First the daimyo signed a pledge of loyalty to the shogun, then they were required to establish a residence in Edo, where the family lived as virtual hostages the whole year round, and where they themselves were obliged to spend every other year. The result was that the resources of the daimyo were to a certain extent drained and rechannelled into the wealth of the new capital, which expanded at an extraordinary rate. The policy effected political control most efficiently, but it also ensured the seclusion of the capital.

The social stability and newly-acquired wealth in the capital produced a great trade boom. The old barter system based on rice was replaced by a money economy, and at the expense of the old daimyo and samurai classes, the merchants amassed great fortunes. Their money was inevitably spent on the pleasures of the city—the popular theatre of Kabuki and the geisha quarters. Consequently the art of the Edo period reflected the taste of the merchant class; it was a popular art, devoid of religious influence. In contrast to its subdued classical counterpart, Noh, with its Buddhist undertones, the Kabuki theatre burst with colour and movement, and provided inspiration for the early woodblock prints, Ukiyo-e, which depicted actors, courtesans and the delights of the 'floating world' of city life. The popular art of Edo was an urban art, nurtured by the comparative isolation from the provinces and the wilder, more remote areas of the country.

Edo was the capital for strategic reasons, not for the natural beauty of its surroundings or their geomantic qualities. The richer daimyo and those in the shogun's court soon started to build large parks on the outskirts of the city. Their parks were on a grand scale and represented the wealth and status of their positions. The landscapes reflected their urban isolation, for they illustrated literary and moral illusions with the use of foreign scenery. They represented an ideal of landscape and expressed the borrowed image. Their design was based on the stroll garden; Katsura provided an elegant model. But with the grandeur of scale the tone of the landscape changed, the colours and shapes became bolder; more conspicuous plant forms such as cyclads (sago palm—Jap. sotetsu) and banks of azaleas were used. Though beautiful in their display, these gardens possessed little of the power once achieved by understatement.

The oldest and finest garden of the period is Koishikawa Koraku-en, which was built by the vice-shogun, Tokugawa Yorifusa, as a place for tea ceremonies on an elaborate, decadent scale. A site was found that included trees and small hills, features most unusual in the Edo area. An estate and two temples were removed to make way for a large and lavish landscape. Work was started in 1629 and tea ceremonies were held the following year. The name 'Koraku-en' was derived from a Confucian text; 'Koraku', meaning 'afterwards, ease', referred to the wise ruler taking his ease only when the country was prosperous and the people contented.

Under the authoritarian rule of the Tokugawas, Japan retreated into isolation; no foreign travel was permitted and no foreigners except for Chinese were allowed to enter the country. At the same time as they warded off the Western merchants and missionaries, they turned once again to the mainland of the continent to find a suitable model on which to build a stable State. Confucianism, with its ethical implications, provided the ideal.

Patronage of Shinto, with its emphasis on the Emperor's divinity, would have threatened the position of the shogun, who was in effect a usurper. The shogun continued to patronise the Buddhist church, which remained the dominant religion but was split by internal differences. Confucianism, with its emphasis on conformity to the State and to rules of proper conduct, reinforced the social hierarchy with the shogun firmly seated at its summit. In 1608 Ieyasu had appointed a Confucian scholar to his court, and an interest in the teachings of the twelfth-century orthodox Confucian, Chu Hsi (Jap. Shushi), was soon fostered. The freedom of Zen was replaced by Confucian morality.

Koraku-en was later developed by Tokugawa Mitsukuni, the son of Yorifusa, under the guidance of a Chinese scholar, Chu Shun Shui (1600–1682), a refugee from the fall of the Ming dynasty. His influence may account for many of the Chinese features of the garden, which include a shrine, Tokujin-do, built by Mitsukuni in 1630 and dedicated to Confucius.

The garden was structured around a lake, which was encircled by a winding path. In the centre of the lake was a large island shaped like a tortoise, with a huge rock rising out of the water, representing the head of the creature. The tortoise, together with the crane, is a creature much admired by the Chinese and Japanese as a symbol of long life; the tortoise stones (kame-ishi or kame-seki) were common features on the banks of garden streams. The tortoise island is a symbol of one of the legendary Chinese 'mystic isles' or 'isles of the blest' (horaijima), which had been introduced into Chinese gardening in the Han dynasty by the Emperor Wu and were adopted in the early Japanese gardens. The Immortals were said to live by the shores of the mystic isles in palaces of jade and precious stones. The islands rose sheer to towering pinnacles of rock; their lower slopes were luxuriously forested with trees that grew pearls; the birds and beasts were pure white. The islands drifted in the ocean until the Supreme One ordered fifteen tortoises to support them on their backs. However, a giant carried off the tortoises and the isles drifted away for ever. They have survived as dreams of paradise to be found in many old garden lakes. Again the image of the garden was symbolic.

By the side of the water a mountain was constructed out of the excavated material from the lake. It rose to a point about thirty feet high and was covered with a small variety of bamboo, sasa. The mountain was named Lu Shan after the mountain in the Kiangsi province of China, where the Amidist monk Hui Yan (334–416) founded the famous White Lotus sect. The garden abounds in other Chinese images; there are hills covered with white azaleas from Loochoo, known as the Loochoo mountains; a miniature model of the dike that crosses Lake Hsi Hu at Hangchow; a lotus pond, Seko-tsutsumi, named after a famous Chinese lake, which is

[89]

spanned by a semi-circular stone bridge, the Engetsu-kyo or Full Moon bridge, since it forms a full circle with its reflection in the water.

Many of the other garden features depict literary allusions or demonstrate a nostalgia for the scenery of the old capital, Kyoto. Like Katsura, Koraku-en could only be fully appreciated with a thorough knowledge of classical literature. The intention was to reproduce models of famous beauty spots and to copy their features. The power of suggestion was replaced by literal representation. Unlike the mandala structure of the paradise gardens, these purely aesthetic stroll gardens presented a series of different scenes which were often unrelated. The views were calculated to impress by their variety, rather than by a cultivated mood achieved through a sequential arrangement around the path. As one jumped from imaginary Chinese scenes to memories of the old capital, it was difficult to form a coherent impression of the garden.

Specific beauty spots were represented by the inclusion of familiar features. At Koraku-en there are two streams: one is modelled on the River Tatsula and its banks are planted with maples for which the river is famous; the other is a shallow stream, its bed strewn with boulders and its banks lined with pebbled shores after the River Oi, Rapid River, in Kyoto. Bridges were important details which provided clues to the identity of the original scenery, and numerous different styles of bridge were used at Koraku-en. An earthen bridge (dobashi), the Togetsu-kyo (named after the bridge at Arashiyama in Kyoto), spans the rocky shallows of the replica River Oi. It was constructed by laying logs across a slightly arched timber framework, then covering the logs with a layer of turf. There are stone bridges made from rough slabs of granite joined in an arch with a mortise and tenon, as if they were timber. Over the iris beds there is a bridge of eight planks arranged in a zig-zag fashion and raised on stakes; it is known as Yatsu-hashi, the Eightfold Bridge. The whole scene has been inspired by the famous eightfold bridge and iris beds in Mikawa province. Many artists were to depict this, notably Ogata Korin (1658–1716) of the Rimpa school, and the Ukiyo-e master Hokusai (1760–1849) in his series of prints illustrating famous bridges, Shokoku

[90]

mekyo kiran (1827–1830). Like the irregular spacing of the stepping-stones of the 'roji', which drew one's concentration, the winding bridge encourages you to linger and then be drawn to the beauty of the flowers.

Among the features of Koraku-en were a pine grove, a plum grove, wistaria trellises, a waterfall, Shiraito-no-taki, a most unusual sight in Edo (in the north-west corner of the garden is a waterwheel and adjoining miller's cottage; the wheel pumps water to the upper storey of the mill, from where it is piped to the top of the Lu Shan mountain, then down to the cascade) and numerous water basins and stone lanterns. The air of rural detachment is suggested not by a tea house, but by a thatched sake house, Kuhachi-ya. Stones were transported from long distances at great expense, since Edo had none of the natural outcrops to be found around Kyoto.

Stones became valuable objects which were bought and sold at high prices; rock merchants were soon established in the capital, and they sent their men out into the country to bring back suitable boulders for the gardens. The art of stones, which was once a means of expressing the image of the immediate landscape, became a means for displaying wealth. Koraku-en contains many rocks and also shrubs that had been clipped and shaped to represent the similar forms of garden hillock and mountain. However, the fundamental balance of the opposites was not ignored, for almost hidden by the undergrowth is the beautiful form of the female stone, in-seki, and in a prominent position under a pine tree, stands the phallic form of the male stone, yo-seki.

The literary garden evidently held great appeal for the daimyo. It was a mark of their erudition and sophistication. Another of the Edo gardens, Rikugien, which still survives in modern Tokyo, was a reconstruction of scenes from the Kokin Wakashu, the Collection of Ancient and Modern Times, a tenth-century anthology of poems. Rikugien contains no less than eighty-eight views derived from the poems; the name itself originates from the same source and refers to six principles of poem composition. Like Koraku-en, this later garden built by a wealthy daimyo, Yanagisawa Yoshiyasu, in 1702, has its standard set-pieces. Covering twenty-five acres, the stroll garden is built around the lake, which

contains 'the mystic isles', horaijima; there is also a Togetsu-kyo bridge and an eightfold bridge along the path.

The extravagant size of both Koraku-en and Riku-gien encompassed a secluded and beautiful world, but the very extravagance of this style and its repetition provided the limitations which were to set the decline of the garden art, for the garden in no way reflected the landscape surrounding Edo. There is, however, a most conspicuous exception. Only fifty miles from the centre of the city is Mount Fuji, the great, snow-capped volcano, which is the core of Japan and the subject of repeated illustration. A fine example of integration of garden design and natural landscape, featuring Mount Fuji, can be seen in Tokyo today at the lake garden of Hama Rikyu. It was the garden of the Imperial Detached Palace during the Meiji period, but it was originally laid out in the late seventeenth century by the daimyo of Kofu province, Matsudaira Tsunashige.

It is an island of ninety-six acres, since three sides are enclosed by a walled canal and the fourth side faces out into Tokyo Bay. Unlike Kyoto, Edo had no abundant supply of water, so the marshy area beside the bay was ideal for building a lake; it could be filled by the rising tide and the water retained by a tidal water gate. On the coastal side of the garden, pine trees were planted and grew to form the twisted, windswept shapes so admired and familiar along the shores of Japan. In one direction your eye travelled from the shore of the garden to the sea itself, and in the other, Mount Fuji could be seen rising in the distance. Both the bay and the volcano had been incorporated into the garden by the technique known as shakkei or 'borrowed scenery', which literally meant 'to capture alive'.

The garden is a world within a world. The Japanese who so skilfully strip the veneer of beauty to find the pure element or the essence of form, delight in the image that is multi-layered. They have applied it to their social conventions and rituals, which to us as Westerners often appear as emotionless performance, when all we are seeing is the surface of their experience and its outward restraint. The ability to perform and express with such simplicity is achieved by the detachment they have developed, for they know how to step outside themselves on a superficial level of experience, and then find themselves on a more profound level. In the same way their artistic sensibility searches for the image which contains form within another form, or experience within experience.

The garden offered detachment and it once projected a multi-layered range of experience. Space (which is so limited due to the topography of Japan), or the illusion of space, could be extended or explored within the separate world of the garden as it could in the painting. But it could be extended still further if the seclusion of the garden could be linked to the distant horizon of the surrounding landscape; if the world inside could relate to the world outside. Shakkei was the bridge.

Shakkei was a principle of composition which had been learned from the landscape painters. The space of their paintings had been defined by the borders of the picture, as the space of Ryoanji had been framed by the enclosing wall, or the space of the pebbled precincts of Ise-jingu had been contained by the wooden fence and surrounding forest. To capture a view of the landscape outside and so extend the illusory space of the garden to the distant horizon, the view had to be framed, then linked to the garden. The subject of the view was usually a mountain or the sea; Hama Rikyu had included both.

The sense of space and depth in the paintings had been created by the vast areas of sky and cloud; the shakkei composition employs the same method by framing an expanse of sky around the mountain. Specific techniques were used for the actual framing: through a break in a line of trees or in a hedge, a glimpse of the spreading landscape could be caught, or a window or pillars in a tea house or pavilion could frame a scene in the distance beyond the garden. Then by placing a garden feature such as a stone lantern, a rock or basin in the foreground in front of the view, the far horizon could be incorporated with the design of the garden. The foreground within the garden was thus linked to the background outside, the composition completed and the sense of distance captured in a single view.

With the stroll gardens of Edo, the garden art had come full circle. As the city rapidly expanded, the space available for large landscapes was diminishing, but the very

lack of space and the urban development only emphasised the need for the garden. The daimyo, who had displayed their wealth in the elaborate parks of the capital, soon found their resources dwindling. The merchant class were forbidden by the government to flaunt openly their newly-accumulated riches, so the stroll garden soon became a memory of past wealth.

One of the great lessons of Japanese gardening was that space could be created and a sense of distance compressed into a few yards. The only area available to the merchants for creating a garden was the courtyard, which was enclosed by the wings of the house. Courtyard gardens had been arranged in the tsubo, the yards between the wings of the Heian shinden mansion, so the merchants were following an old tradition. The yard was covered with coarse sand or moss, which was frequently sprinkled with water, so as to appear damp and fresh. Flowering plants were unsuitable for the dark shade of the yard and they would have clashed with the flowers arranged inside the house, so they were avoided. With the exception of the maple, deciduous trees were also avoided, and small palms, bamboo and shrubs such

[95]

as azalea, daphne (*odera* and *retusa*; Jap. Jinchoge) and camellia were used. Stepping-stones, water basins and stone lanterns were also common, though their function was purely ornamental.

Elements of the courtyard garden were borrowed from the tea garden and the dry landscape, though little of their significance was realised by the city merchants. The small courtyard garden has survived in the modern Japanese city to bring relief and offer a sense of calm in the centre of the noise and rush of modern, urban life. It still retains something of the transitional function of the tea garden, for after closing the gate on the outside world, you pass through the garden before moving into the detached privacy of the house itself. Though the garden once provided the detachment necessary to focus more clearly on transient natural beauty, in the context of the modern city it provides escape. Whereas the garden once revealed how closely men had merged themselves with Nature, the city garden exposes how far they have travelled in the opposite direction. The one suggests an intuitive knowledge, the other betrays a naïve ignorance.

The Tokugawa era was a period of repression. With the influence of Confucianism came the growth of formalism; free, inspired creation became incomprehensible. The great gardens of the past could only be reinterpreted within the confines of categories and the contemporary gardens were designed according to a rigid formula. A well-known courtier of the time was quoted as saying, 'the garden of Ryoanji is beyond my understanding. I do not know whether it is good or not, but there is something superior about it,' and when referring to the sand garden of Daisen-in at Daitokuji, he said, 'there are some things about it I cannot understand, but certain rules seem to have been followed'.★

★ See Lorraine Kuck: *The World of the Japanese Garden.*

The gardener families of the Muromachi period passed down their techniques from generation to generation, and guarded them with the mystique of secrecy, but the techniques lasted longer than the original inspiration. When the garden became a sign of wealth, the art became a business; when rocks exchanged hands at high prices, the gardener no longer expressed a vision, but designed a product.

The Sakuteiki and other old texts on gardens, based on the geomantic tradition, were republished during the Tokugawa era. The geomantic principles, which represented an archaic imagery, were interpreted as rules as they were during the Heian period. Gardens were then classified as 'hill garden' (tsukiyama niwa), 'flat garden' (hira niwa) and 'the garden attached to tea house' (chaniwa), and each style had three forms or degrees of finish, 'elaborate' (shin), 'intermediate' (gyo) and 'rough' (so). These categories were unimaginatively adhered to and the spontaneity that had characterised the Zen spirit was replaced by dogma, for the geomantic image was as incomprehensible as the abstraction of landscape.

The growth of Edo symbolised the birth of a great, commercial nation. The prosperity of the business enterprises marked the rise of a new order. Both the seclusion of Edo and the urban expansion generated fresh attitudes and a new creative spirit, but they also signified the severing of certain links with the past and the loss of a particular identity. The garden mirrored this change most clearly, for the inspiration of the Edo gardens was found in literature; the image of landscape was no longer direct, it was borrowed and second-hand. The literary allusion replaced the vision of landscape and what was once achieved with ease and simplicity, became elaborate and contrived. The garden was divorced from the land.

Back to the Volcano

Japan is a country of extremes; a newly-risen land that shudders from the molten core of the volcano, then unrolls down soft, forested hills to the fertile plain. Its piercing, thrusting forms can be delicate and gentle; its mood can change abruptly from tropical storms or Siberian wind to a still calm in an autumn light. The oriental attitude can accommodate such clearly-defined changes with a quiet acceptance, when we as Westerners might see only contradictions. It may seem unrealistic to describe the imagination of a people attuned to an inherent, natural harmony, when devastation and pollution characterise much of modern Japan. But Japan, like the garden, contains a world within a world; beside the expansion of an industrial society and the growth of an economic superpower, there remains a spirit close to the pulse of Nature, which has not been divorced from the native landscape. Behind the façade, there is an awareness that is constant and can be experienced if one turns off the main highways of Japan, away from the cities and back to the mountains, the forests and the coast.

That detachment which enabled men to become one with Nature, also allowed them to stand aside from the flow. Once severed from the land and their past source of identity, they learned to fear Nature and to control it. It is a short step from detachment to disregard, and from passive acceptance to indifference. The bending form of the garden pine tree can appear tortured and tormented.

It would be simple to claim that as a result of urbanisation, it was inevitable that a past vision should become incomprehensible. But the decline of the garden art was not due to the growth of Edo alone; Kyoto still flourished as a cultural centre and traditional skills were still alive. Having come full circle, the gardens could be refined no further without moving away from the original inspiration. Like a sculptor 'hollowing space' to uncover a perfect form, if a certain critical stage is passed and the hollowing process continued, the image is lost. The image can be reduced so far, then subsequent reduction is movement in the opposite direction—a distortion of the image.

When over-refined, an art can be cut adrift from its source. The artist cannot afford to set distances between himself and his work, he must move and grow with his creation to maintain its vitality. By following the way of Zen, the Muromachi artists had projected themselves into their landscapes, allowing themselves to be engulfed in their deep valleys, and closed the gap between the artist and his creation. Having reached that stage of identification when the artist became one with his work, he acted as the agent through which the art took form, not as the creator moulding form to suit his own design.

Although the gardener talked of 'capturing a scene alive' and the painter spoke of 'capturing the movement of the spirit', their art was an art of release, not constraint. There is no formula to an inspired work of art, but the gardeners of the Tokugawa period believed the art could be refined to a simple code of rules, and that by controlling natural form they could capture the image. To satisfy the daimyo, they designed gardens according to a rigid pattern, and in so doing they froze the image.

The tradition of Nature aesthetics continues. The different schools of tea flourish; young ladies practise the ceremony in order to cultivate proper etiquette and elegance; the ritual is perfected but little of its power is grasped. The performance survives but its detachment is as remote as a mountain hut by a busy roadside.

As to paint bamboo it was necessary to become bamboo, the gardener likewise became part of the garden. He selected the natural forms about him, so as to uncover their beauty. He was not taming Nature, he was unleashing it. But as soon as that sense of identity was lost, he became an agent exterior to the garden. The pruning of the branches and the shaping of the trees became the contortion and control of natural form. Once divorced from Nature, we learn to fear it. The destruction of the landscape suggests the act of men who are afraid.

There are many lessons to be learned from the gardens that are not concerned with aesthetics, but with the attitudes that underlie them. Now more than ever we cannot afford to neglect the value of such expression. The balance of the garden, inseparable from the rhythm of the landscape, cannot be equated with an art alone. There is a current of which that balance is part, that runs

through the heart of Japan, deeper than an economic miracle. There is a seed of an identity that cannot be washed away even in the chaos of a technological nightmare. The garden, and the intuitions it contains, provides a key to that source.

To move from the exterior of Japan to the centre, to obtain some insight into that vague inner world often clouded by Western interpretations of Zen and to find the inspiration for the garden, one has to travel out into the country itself, to the mountains and the rice fields, the forests and the volcanoes.

I had been travelling for several months, wandering from village to village, and found myself on a journey that seemed to go back into time. I had seen much of the beauty of Kyoto, walked through the temples of Nara, followed paths across the plains of Asuka past the tumuli of the ancient Emperors. I travelled light and slept in the houses of farmers and fishermen, in the open fields and hills, as I moved down to the southern tip of Kyushu where the Shinto tradition is strongest.

I was on a boat heading for a line of small, volcanic islands south of Kyushu, when the sea was suddenly whipped into a violent storm. The boat made for the shelter of the nearest island and we had to disembark on to a small fishing boat and ride the surf into the harbour. When we reached the land, a young man who had been steering the fishing boat beckoned me to follow him. We scrambled over the rough, volcanic lava of the shore, until we reached a small shack built from

drift-wood, that rested in the rocks above a great cave. Inside his hut were the essentials of his existence—some tools and a lamp. In one corner of the hut was a pile of books; he seized one and started to tear the pages from the binding to make a fire. He said he had once read it, and as the flames were licking the paper, I noticed the title page; it was Dostoevsky's *The Idiot*. In the light of the fire I looked across the hut to see a picture of a laughing sage nailed to the wall.

'Who is that?' I asked

'Han-Shan,' he replied, smiling.

In the morning I woke to the shudder of the volcano—a deep booming that seemed to emerge from the ground beneath my feet. I walked out from the hut and sat on the rock facing an expanse of still sea. I turned, and behind me the mist and the rain of the storm had cleared to reveal the volcano, rising from the steaming forest and falling away again sheer to the sea. Below me, my friend was singing in his cave. The volcano continued to growl like a great animal stirring in its sleep. I looked out again into that vast space of ocean and realised I too had come full circle; I had started my journey at a point in space and if ever there was a destination, it was at this random point rising from the sea.

There was no thought of identity, and no need to create space. It was the realisation of the image itself. The sense of a meaningless, timeless moment was caught on the periphery of the world, in the heart of the image. The garden leads one to sense that moment. You start to sense it in the fields, in the mountains, in the sea and in yourself.

Japan a great stone garden in the sea.
Echoes of hoes and weeding,
Centuries of leading hill-creeks down
To ditch and pool in fragile knee-deep fields.
Stone-cutter's chisel and a whanging saw,
Leafy sunshine rustling on a man
Chipping a foot-square rough hinoki beam;
I thought I heard an axe chop in the woods
It broke the dream; and woke up dreaming on a train.
It must have been a thousand years ago
In some old mountain sawmill of Japan.
A horde of excess poets and unwed girls
And I that night prowled Tokyo like a bear
Tracking the human future
Of intelligence and despair.

Gary Snyder

From *Riprap*.

Bibliography

*Conder, Josiah, *Landscape Gardening in Japan*: New York, Dover Publications Inc., 1964

*Kuck, Lorraine, *The World of the Japanese Garden*: New York and Tokyo, John Weatherhill Inc., 1968

*Itoh, Teiji, *The Japanese Garden: An Approach to Nature*: New Haven, London, Tokyo, Yale University Press, 1972

Itoh, Teiji, *Space and Illusion in the Japanese Garden*: New York and Tokyo, John Weatherhill Inc., 1972

Itoh, Teiji, *The Roots of Japanese Architecture*: New York and Tokyo, Harper and Row, 1963

Terukazu, Akiyama, *Japanese Painting*: Lausanne, Editions D'Art Albert Skira, 1961

Reischauer, Edwin, *Japan: The Story of a Nation*: Rutland, Vermont and Tokyo, Charles E. Tuttle Co. Inc., 1970

Storry, Richard, *A History of Modern Japan*: Penguin, 1960

Paine, Robert and Soper, Alexander, *The Art and Architecture of Japan*: Penguin, 1955

*Murasaki, Lady Shikibu, *The Tale of Genji*: transl. Waley, Arthur, London, George Allen and Unwin Ltd., 1933

*Waley, Arthur, transl. *The No Plays of Japan*: London, George Allen and Unwin Ltd., 1920

*Shonagon, Sei, *The Pillow Book of Sei Shonagon*: transl. Morris, Ivan, Oxford University Press, 1967

*Morris, Ivan, *The World of the Shining Prince*: Oxford University Press, 1964

Watts, Alan, *The Way of Zen*: New York, Pantheon Books, 1957

*Suziki, Daisetz, *Zen and Japanese Culture*: Princeton University Press, 1957

*Suziki, Daisetz, *An Introduction to Zen Buddhism*: New York, Grove Press Inc., 1964

*Okakura, Kakuzo, *The Book of Tea*: New York, Dover Publications Inc., 1964

Needham, Joseph, *Science and Civilisation in China* Vol. II: Cambridge University Press, 1956

Eitel, Rev. J., *Feng-Shui*: Cambridge, Cokaygne, 1973

Wilhelm, Helmut, *Eight Lectures on the I Ching*: Princeton University Press, 1973

*Snyder, Gary, *Cold Mountain Poems*: New York, Evergreen Review, 1958

Riprap: Ashland, Mass., Origin Press, 1959

A Range of Poems: London, Fulcrum Press, 1966

*Mishima, Yukio, *Sun and Steel*: Tokyo and Palo Alto, California, Kodansha International, 1970

Eliade, Mircea, *Myths, Dreams and Mysteries*: Glasgow, Fontana Books Ltd., 19—

Mandelstam, Osip, *Selected Essays*: Texas University Press, 1977

Marco Polo, *The Travels*: transl. R. E. Latham, London, Penguin, 1958

Kamo no Chomei, *Hojoki*: from Anthology of Japanese Literature: transl. Keene, Donald, New York, Grove Press, 1955